FREEING ARCHITECTURE

LIXIL Publishing

FREEING ARCHITECTURE

JUNYA ISHIGAMI

Fondation*Cartier*
pour l'art contemporain

Just imagine how many more kinds
of architecture there could be.

Seeing the whole world,
arriving in different places,
connecting with so many people,
all in an instant.

All this is now becoming possible.

Encountering all kinds of individuals.

All kinds of groups.
All kinds of things.
All kinds of environments.
All kinds of values.

Things we know, things we don't.

Architecture receptive
to all of these is rare.

When it comes to the innumerable
things of this world,
the innumerable demands
and challenges of this world,
perhaps we need to interpret
architecture more freely.
Approach it more openly.

Freely as in relaxing more,
being our natural selves.

The kind of freedom that allows
us to conceive of so many more
kinds of architecture,
allowing us to make
diverse choices naturally
and comfortably.

Identifying the right structure
for the location,
flexibly, unbound by
architectural conventions,
each time seriously,
yet simply.

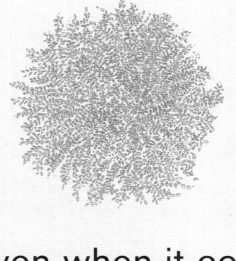

Even when it comes
to building a house,
approaching the task
in a more relaxed fashion,
trusting your own senses,
thinking in terms of
what is accessible,
within reach for you.

Approaching it as if
you were putting together
a garden, a little at a time.

House with Plants

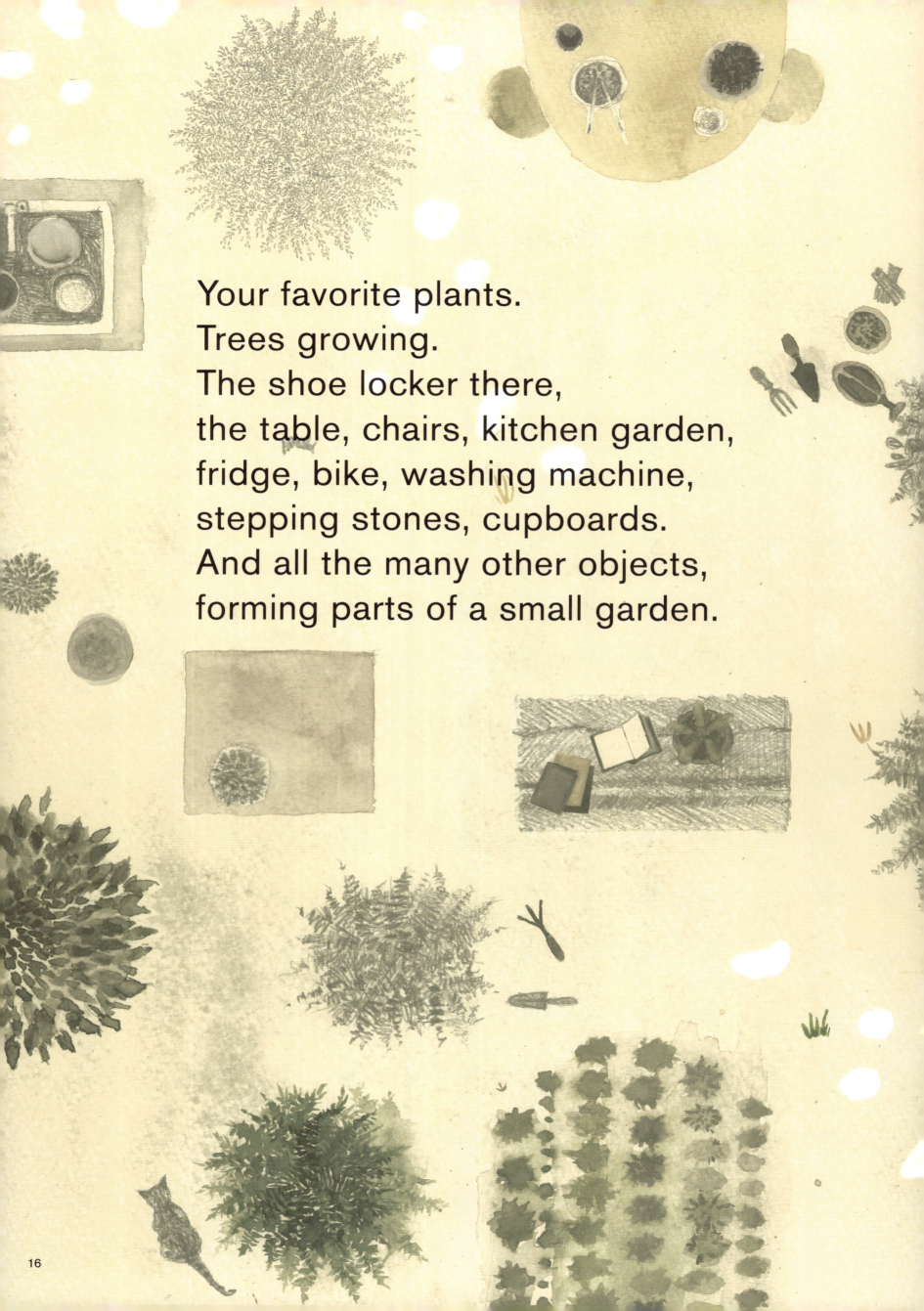

Your favorite plants.
Trees growing.
The shoe locker there,
the table, chairs, kitchen garden,
fridge, bike, washing machine,
stepping stones, cupboards.
And all the many other objects,
forming parts of a small garden.

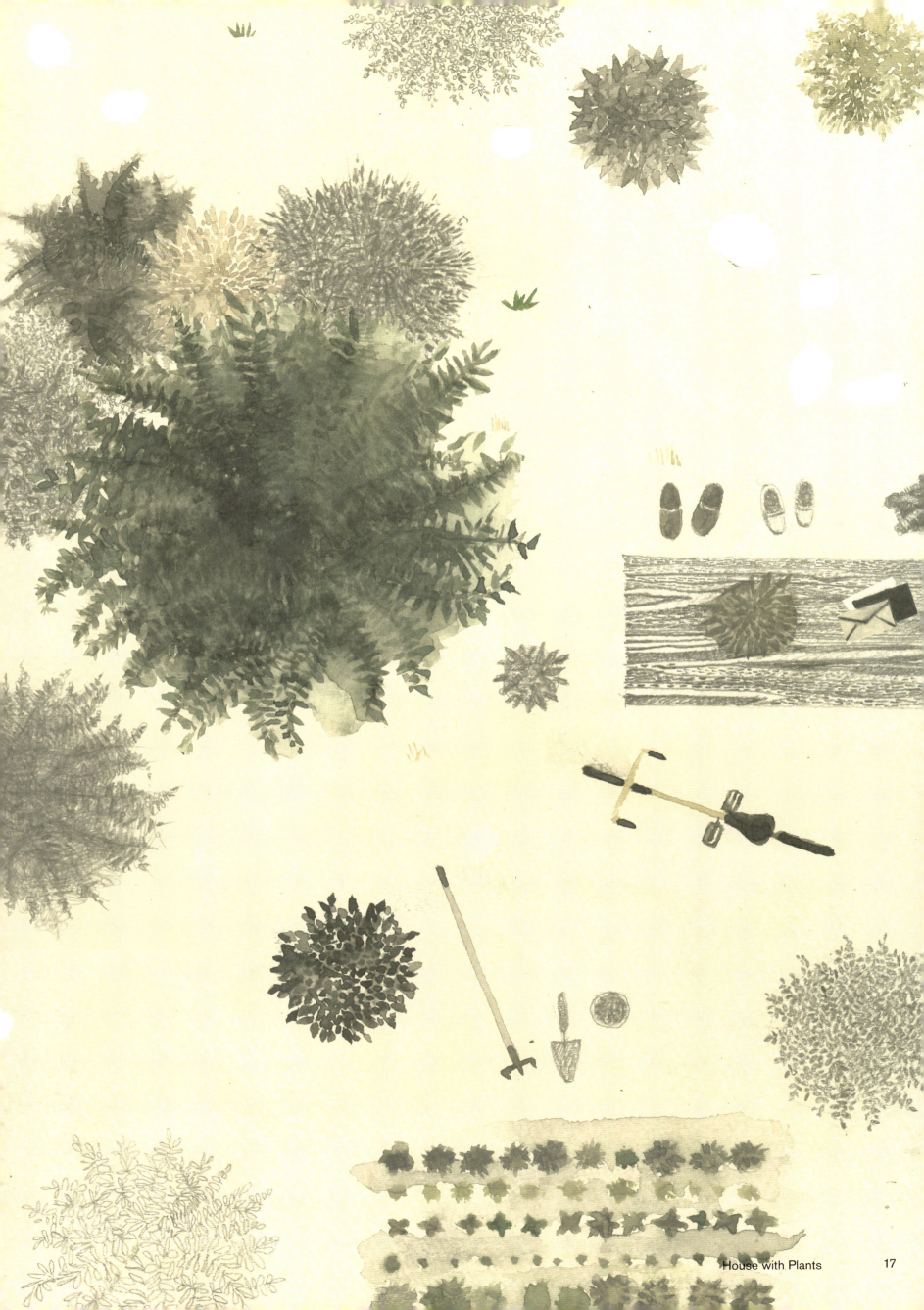
House with Plants

Gardens inside the house and out. Thinking about the view, the scenery, as you go about daily life.

Scenery so modest
as to hardly constitute
architecture.
The idea is to create
within everyday life
this kind of
personal-scale openness,
a product of
individual experience:
an accumulation
of such mini-landscapes
in different places.

Imagine every day,
a world that will
never be complete,
and you can spend
your life dreaming.

House with Plants 23

House with Plants 25

House with Plants 27

There is a forest
I gaze upon all the time.

Very large, but I know
every corner of it well,
as a space
that fits me perfectly.

Here we have a meadow.
Around it, woodland.
Once, it was paddy fields.

A stream flows nearby.
The sluice gate is still there.
Further back in time,
it was mossy forest,
just like the surroundings.

Here a garden will be created.

Botanical Farm Garden Art Biotcp / Water Garden

Next to the meadow is forest.
A woodland I know well.

Here a hotel will be built.
The trees of the forest
will be cut down.

Botanical Farm Garden Art Biotcp / Water Garden

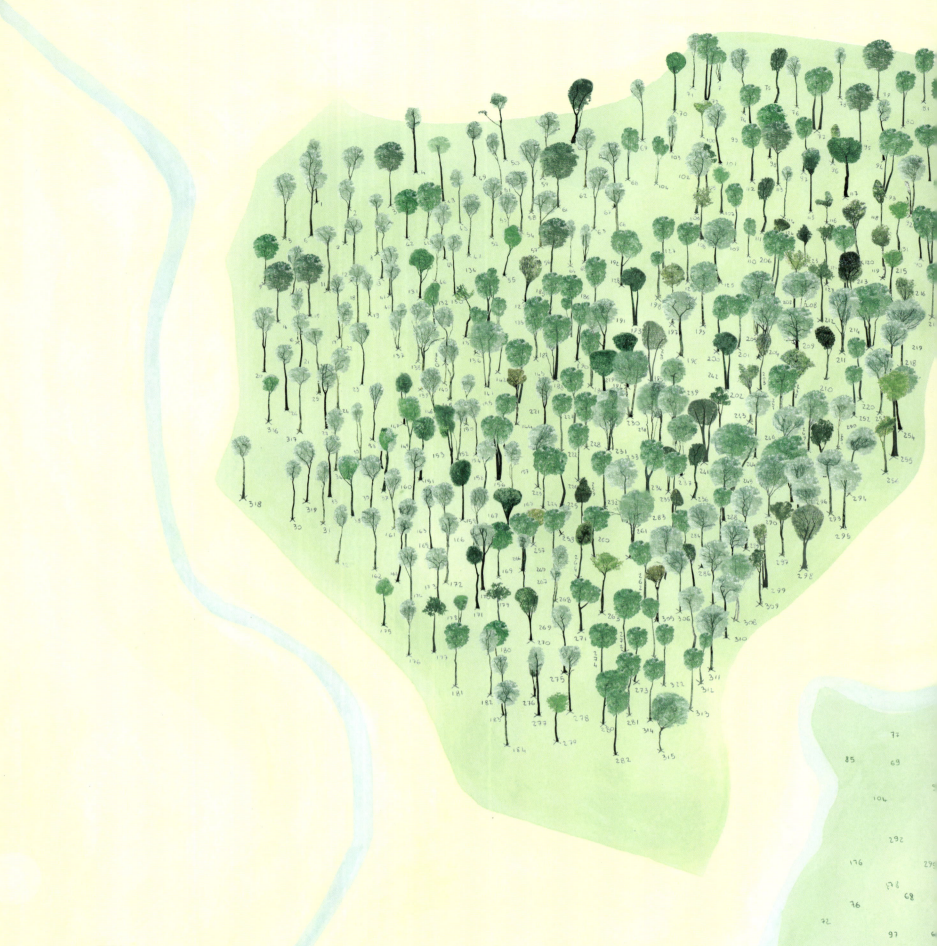

The site where the building will stand occupies the same area as the meadow.

The adjacent forest will be moved in its entirety to the meadow.

Botanical Farm Garden Art Biotcp / Water Garden

Each individual tree of that familiar forest is carefully observed and measured.

Then carefully moved to the adjacent site.

Trees akin to old friends are given a new home. And new relationships.

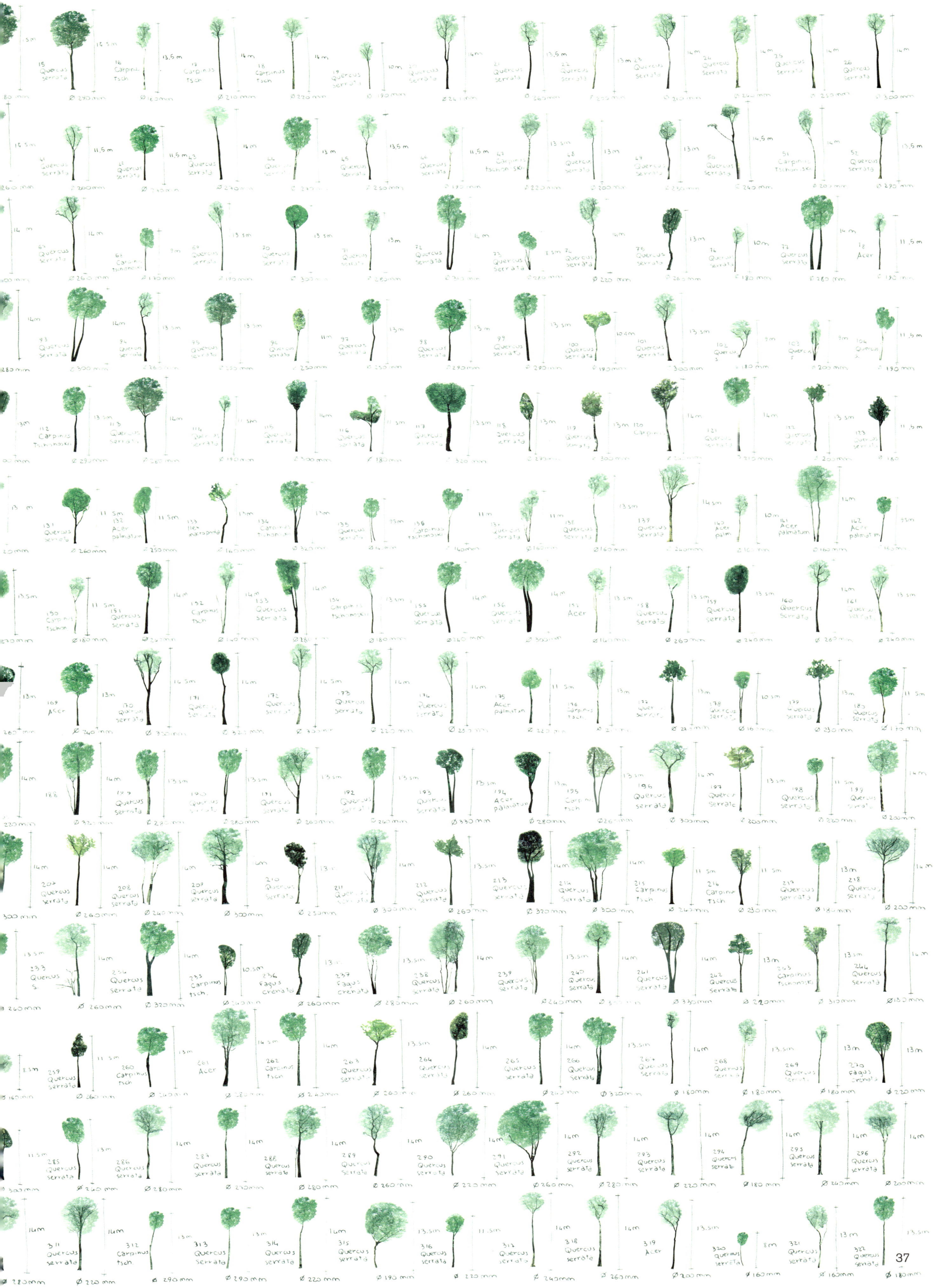

Here the original landscape
is formed,
layer by layer.

Forest.
Paddy fields.
Moss.

Botanical Farm Garden Art Biotop / Water Garden

Water is drawn in
through the sluice gate,
circulates through all the ponds,
and returns to the stream.

All the trees, all the ponds,
a vast forested space,
come together on a personal level.

Each element carefully allotted
a new location.

Landscapes that were originally here,
but never met,
mix and mingle with each other.

Making a new natural environment,
that was not in the original
natural environment,
without using anything new,
and without discarding anything
that was here.

Botanical Farm Garden Art Biotop / Water Garden

Stepping stones are arranged
in the way I suggest
spending time in this place.
Abstracting and recording
my experience here.

No matter how massive the space,
always thinking of it
on an individual scale.

A lovely area of parkland,
historically important,
protected diligently
by a heritage committee.

A landscape that has been here,
unchanging,
for a very long time,
and will remain.

Park Groot Vijversburg Visitor Center

No felling or moving
of existing trees.
No altering the shape
of existing green space.
No demolishing
of existing buildings.

I stroll around the paths.

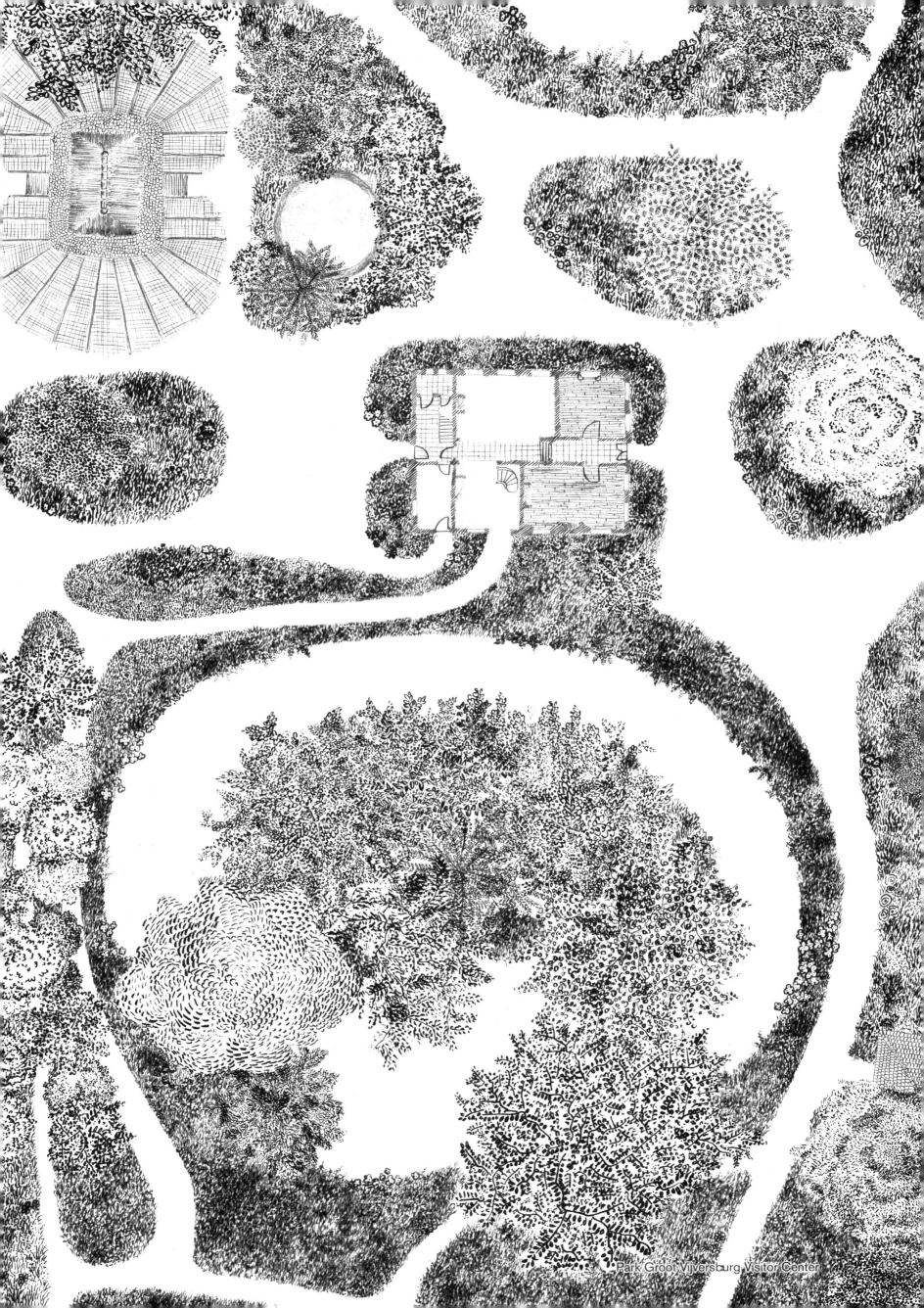

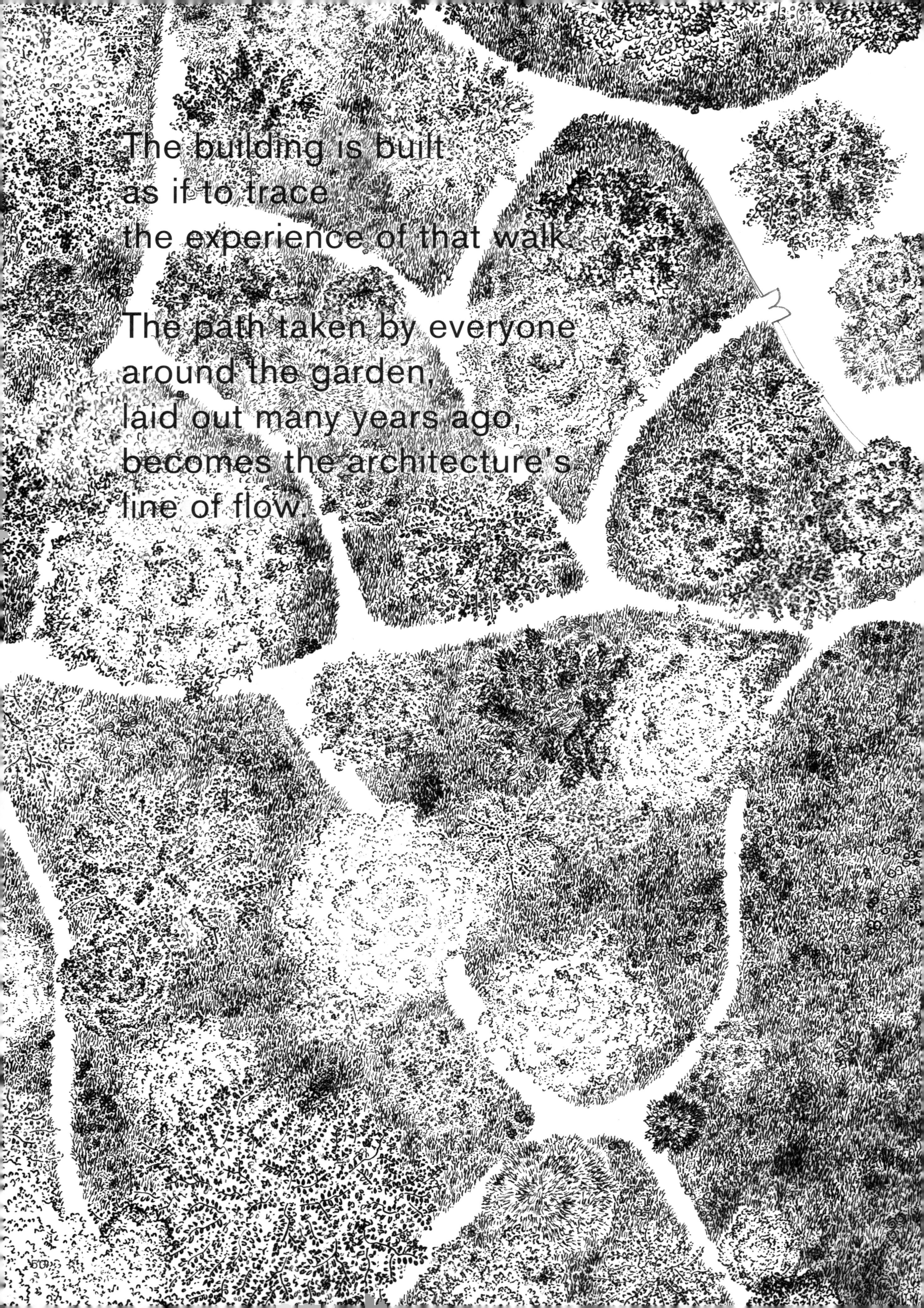

The building is built
as if to trace
the experience of that walk

The path taken by everyone
around the garden,
laid out many years ago,
becomes the architecture's
line of flow

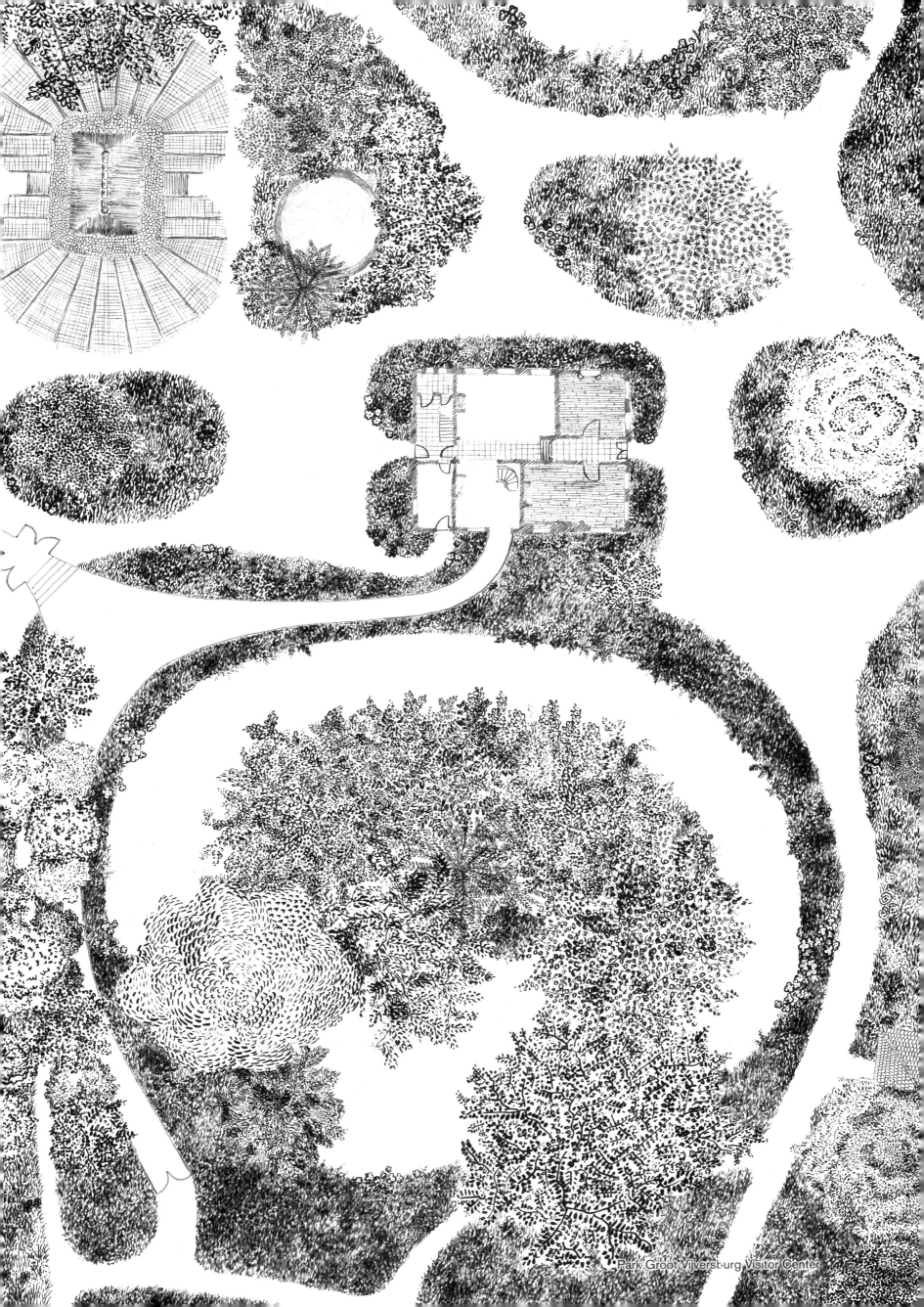

Park Groot Vijversburg Visitor Center

Finding spaces buried
in the landscape.
Architecture
does not create spaces.
Architecture is
merely the beginning.
Where possible,
eliminate its presence.

Park Groot Vijversburg Visitor Center

There are no pillars. Transparent screens trace the environment and bear all the load.

Park Groot Vijversbu g Visitor Center

Environments people do not enter
are left as is,
and from those they do enter
a place is chosen.
Just chosen, that's all.
Footpath becomes space.

Park Groot Vijversburg Visitor Center

In some sections,
the transparent screens
enveloping the space overlap
to form a single sheet.
The interior space is absorbed
into a single pane of glass,
and disappears into the forest.
Becoming, as it vanishes,
architecture.

Park Groot Vijversburg Visitor Center

Discovering spaces
in a beautiful,
unchanging landscape.
Making nothing,
simply finding what is there.
Making structures
is about discovering new worlds.

Park Groot Vijversburg Visitor Center

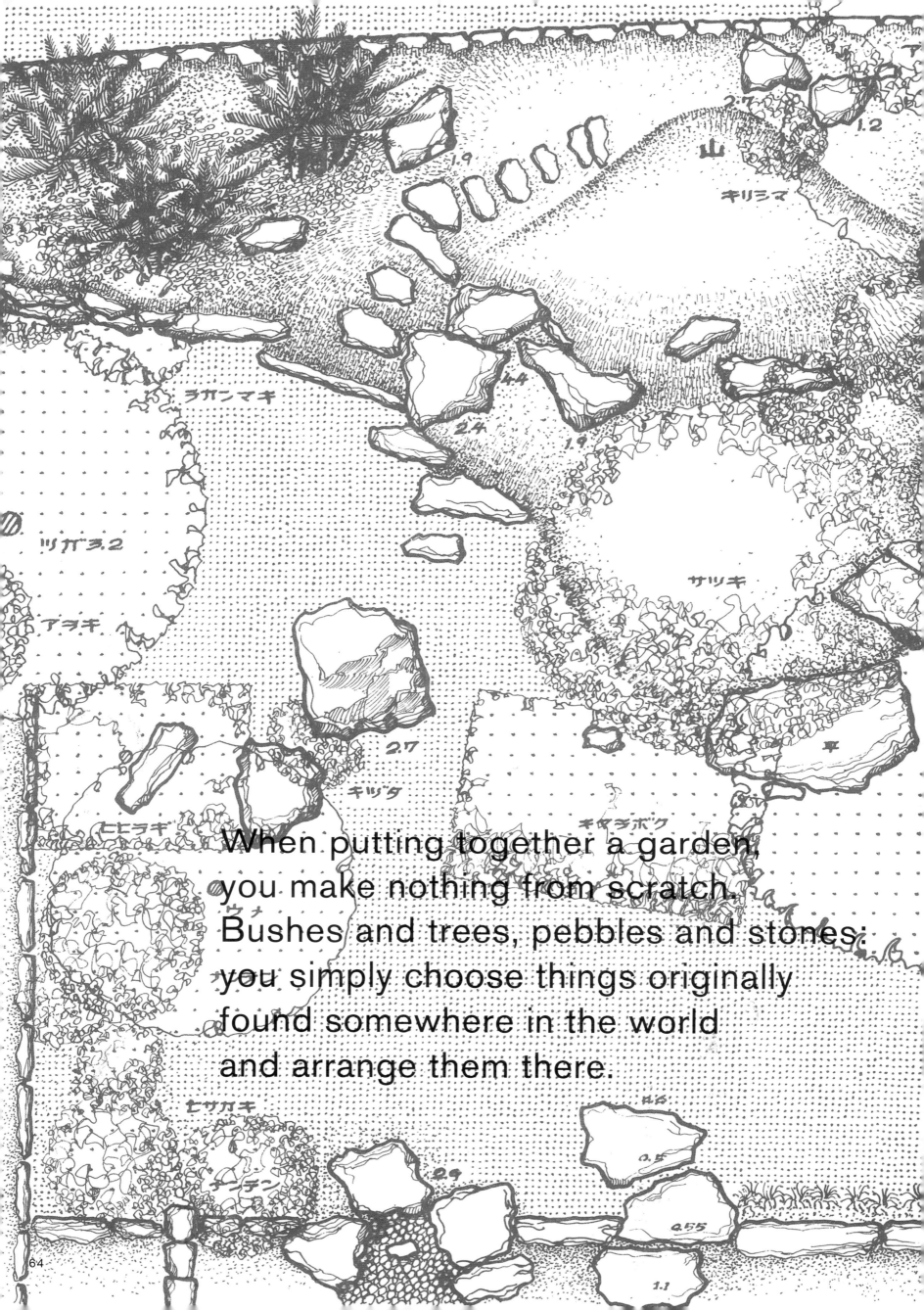

When putting together a garden, you make nothing from scratch. Bushes and trees, pebbles and stones: you simply choose things originally found somewhere in the world and arrange them there.

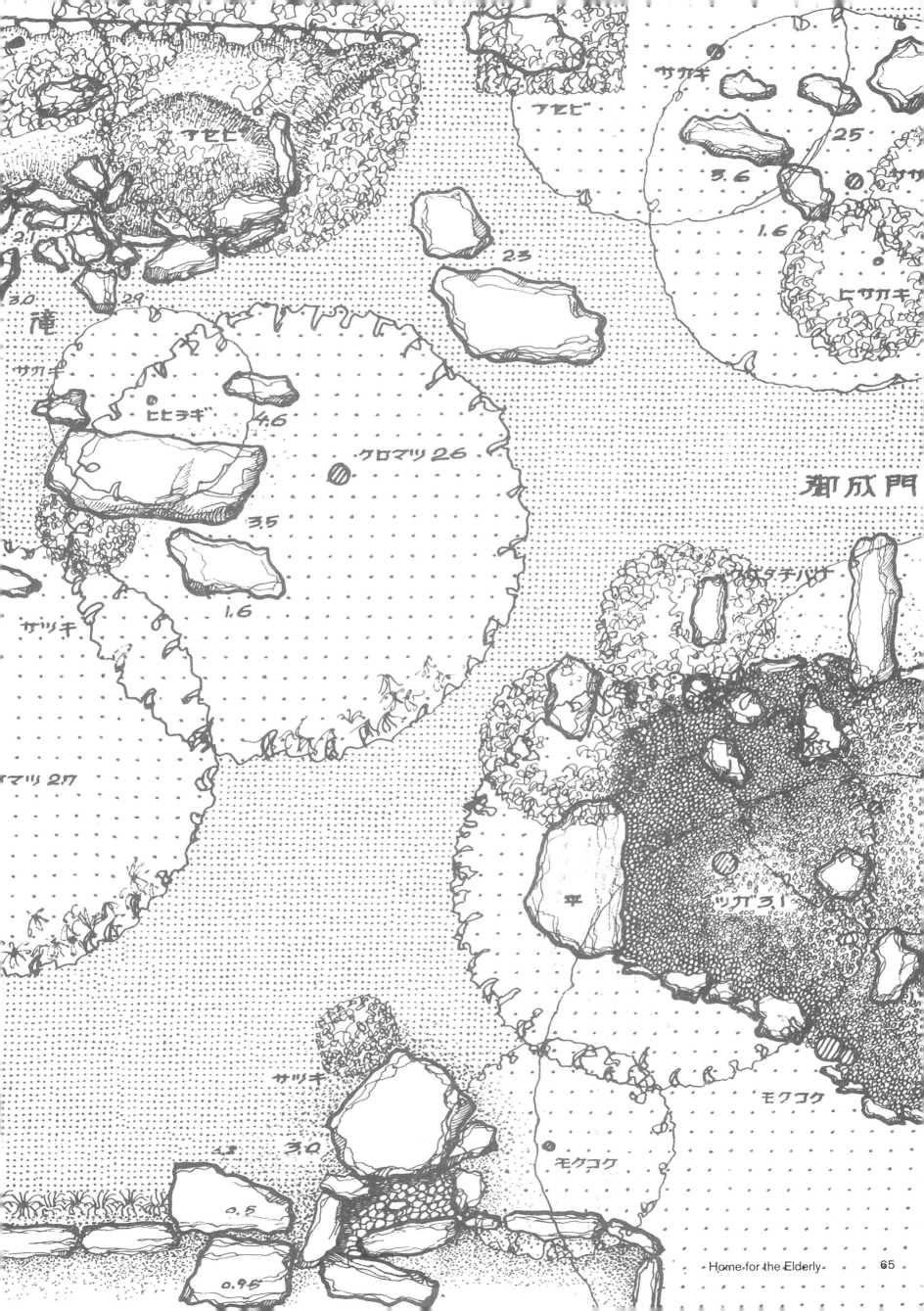
Home for the Elderly

Age is one value
architects cannot create.
Here are floor plans
of old houses from different areas,
all due for demolition.
Era, region, carpenter, resident,
changes over time:
so many variations on each.

The idea was to gather these,
like you might gather flowers
or trees or stones,
and make one big house,
in the way you might
make a garden.

Home for the Elderly

Parts of different houses
are removed,
and collected on-site
to form one large house,
communal accommodation
for elderly dementia patients.

Spaces with different
characteristics
are assembled
so that the residents
will remember them.

Put together in a way
that is not unnatural.
So that the differences
between places
manifest naturally.

Home for the Elderly

Home for the Elderly

Once a house
is dismantled,
the indeterminate
charms and ambience
of age
cannot be recreated,
even if the house
is reassembled.
So the houses
are transported
as they are to the site.

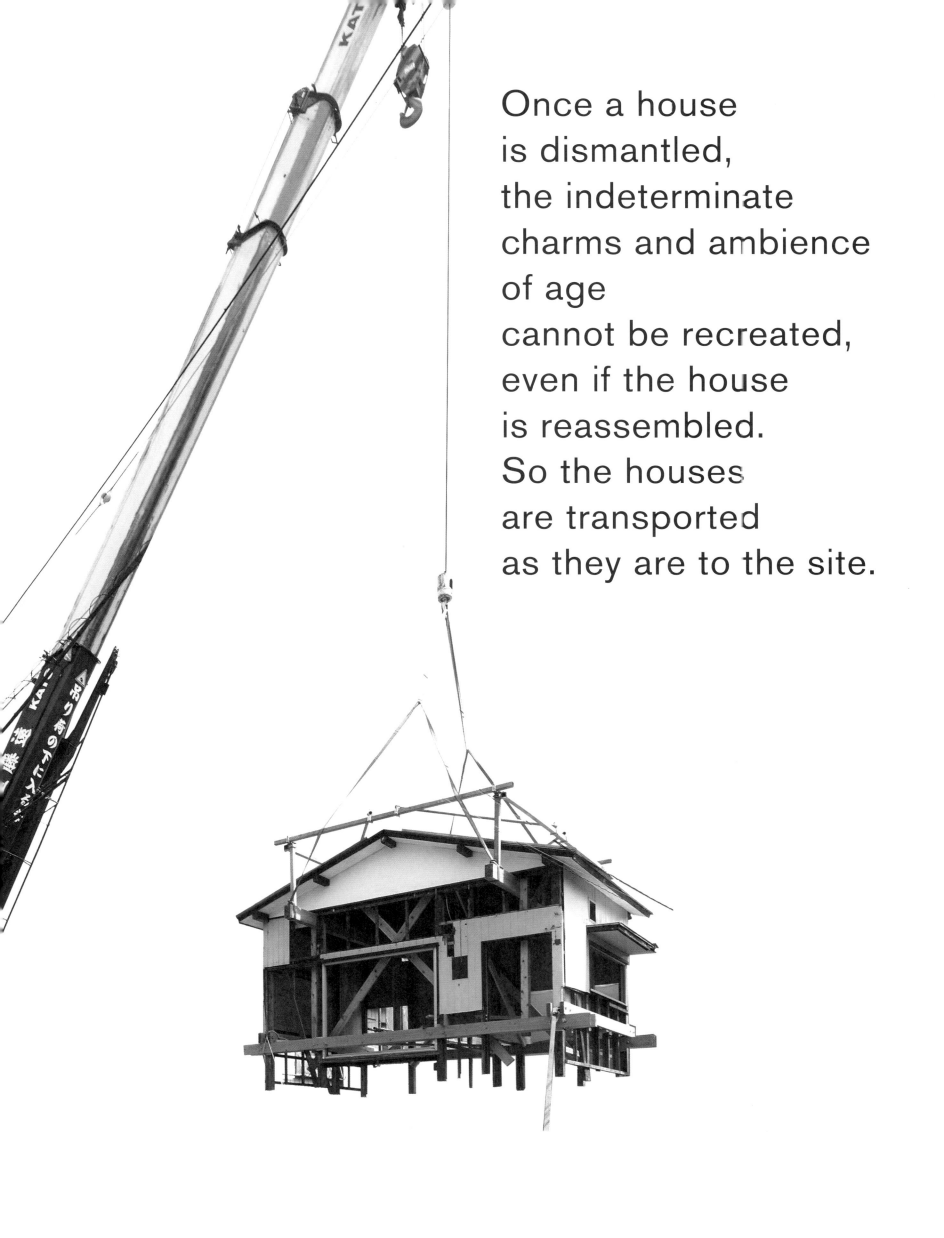

Home for the Elderly 73

Only when gathered on-site can they be viewed together. Gradually a new overall picture begins to form.

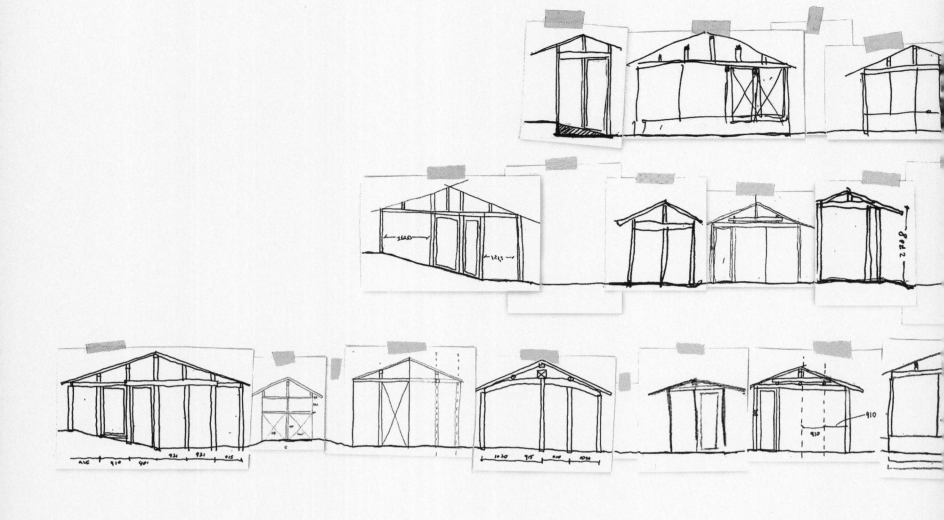

A survey is made of the buildings,
and drawings generated.
These are combined
to form a new structure.
As if joining a series
of unknown worlds
to make a single, new world.

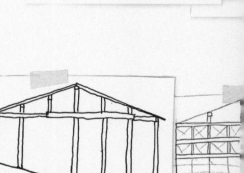

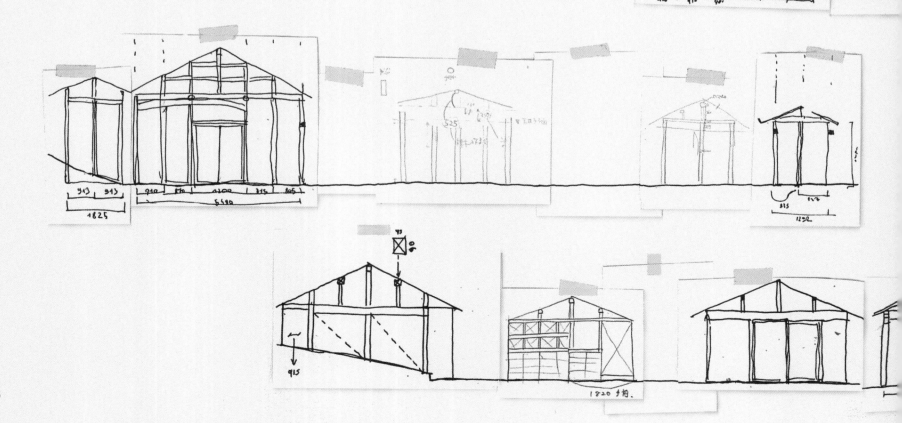

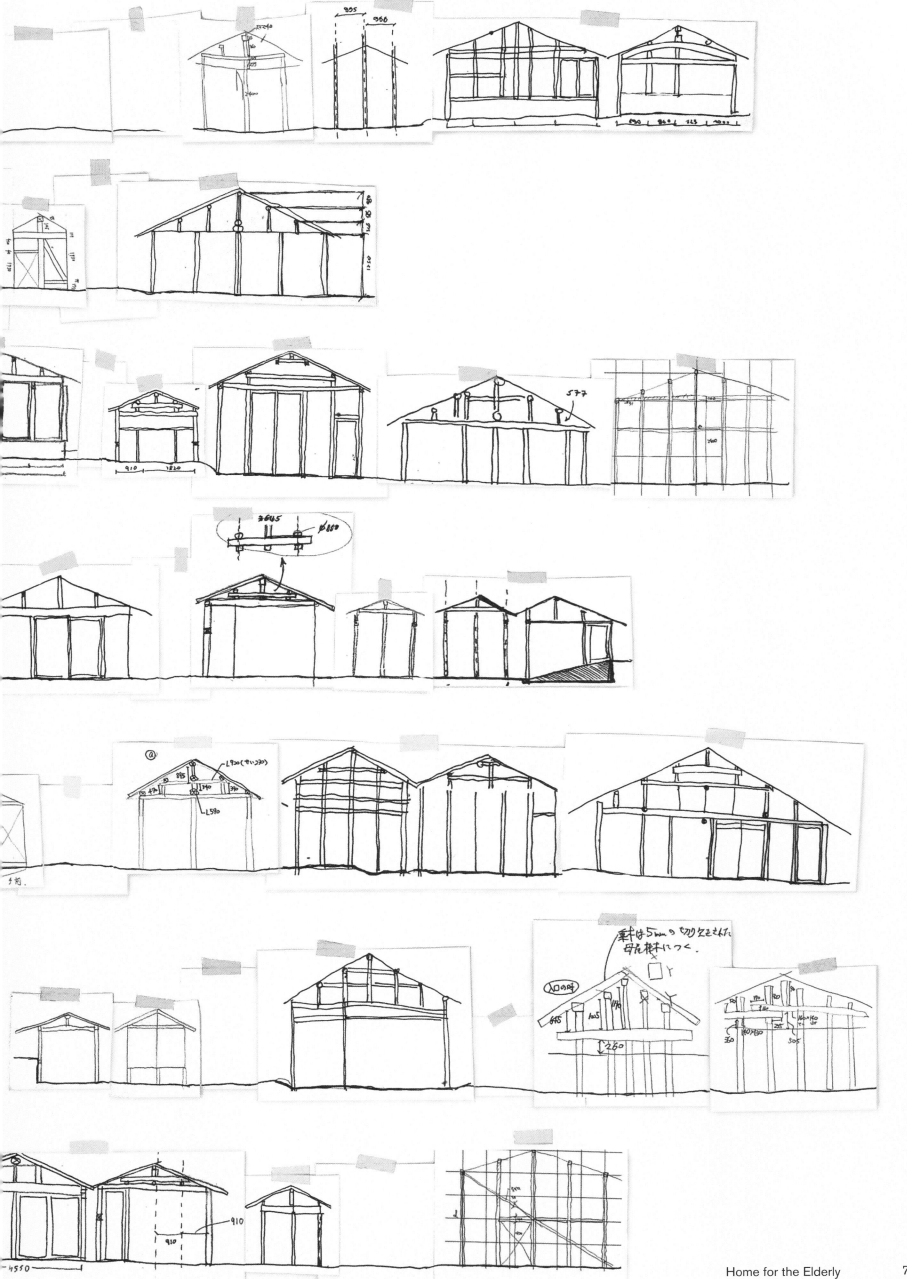

Home for the Elderly

The collected houses are formed
into a single structure.
All the cladding is stripped off,
leaving just the frames.

The framing of wooden buildings
is very attractive,
and highly individual.

Home for the Elderly

Home for the Elderly　83

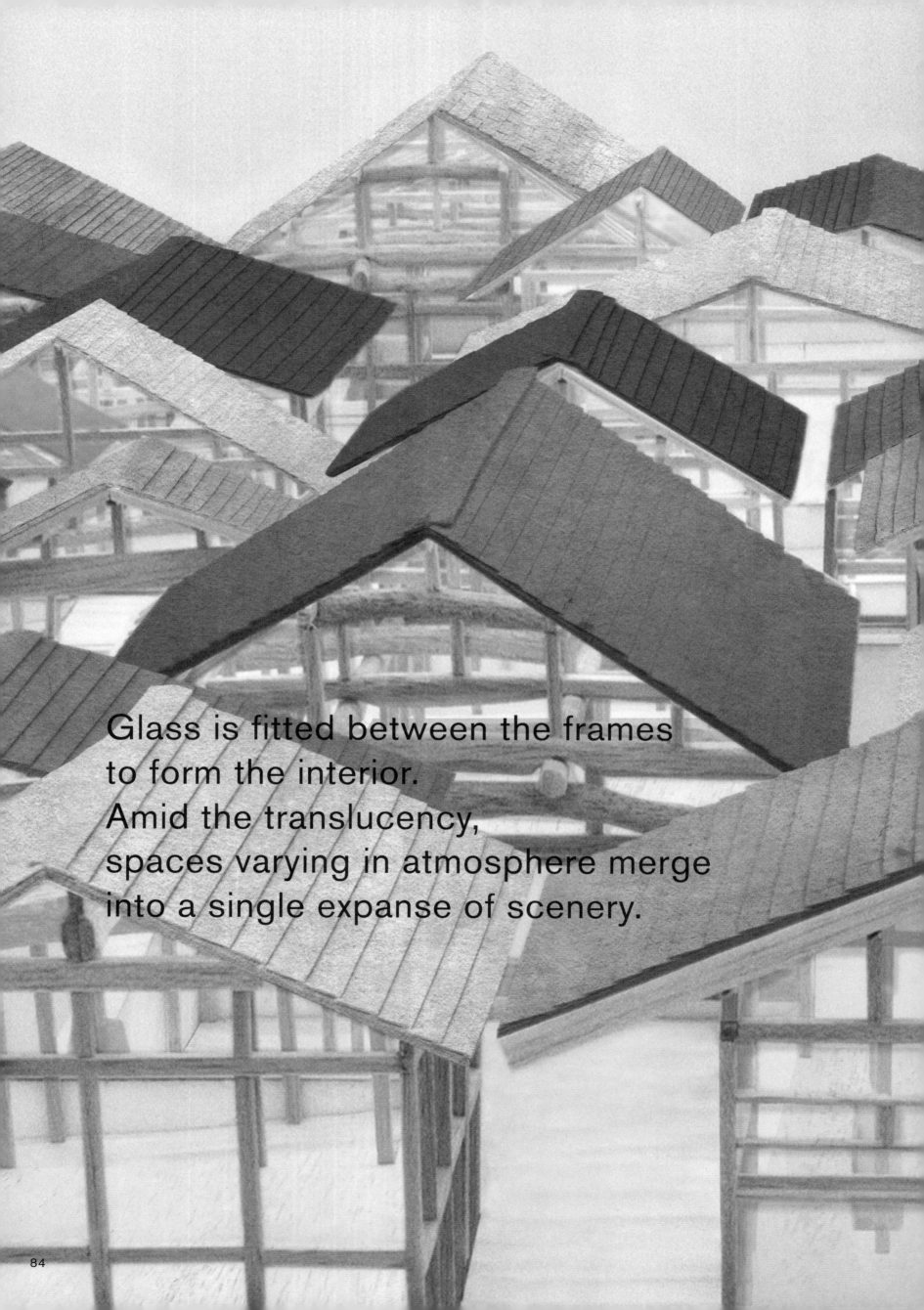

Glass is fitted between the frames
to form the interior.
Amid the translucency,
spaces varying in atmosphere merge
into a single expanse of scenery.

Home for the Elderly

As they go about their lives here,
elderly dementia patients will
naturally start to remember
the subtle characteristics of the spaces:
the state of the framing,
the appearance of the pillars,
the damage and warping,
the way colors have faded.

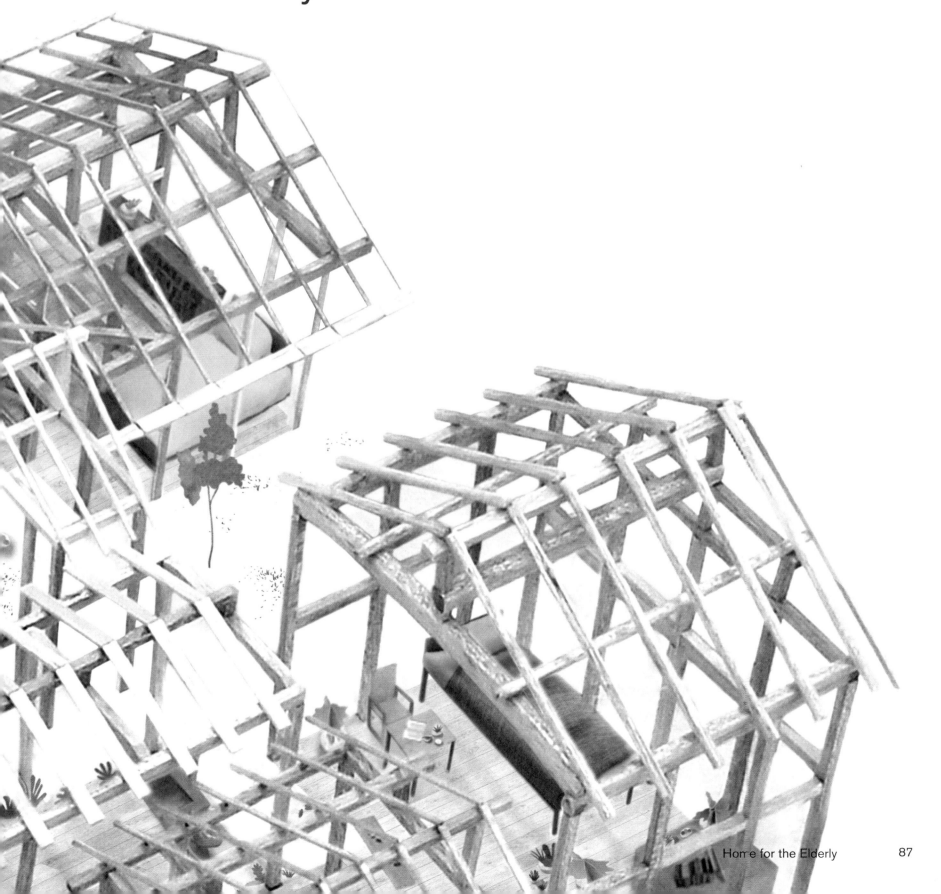

Home for the Elderly

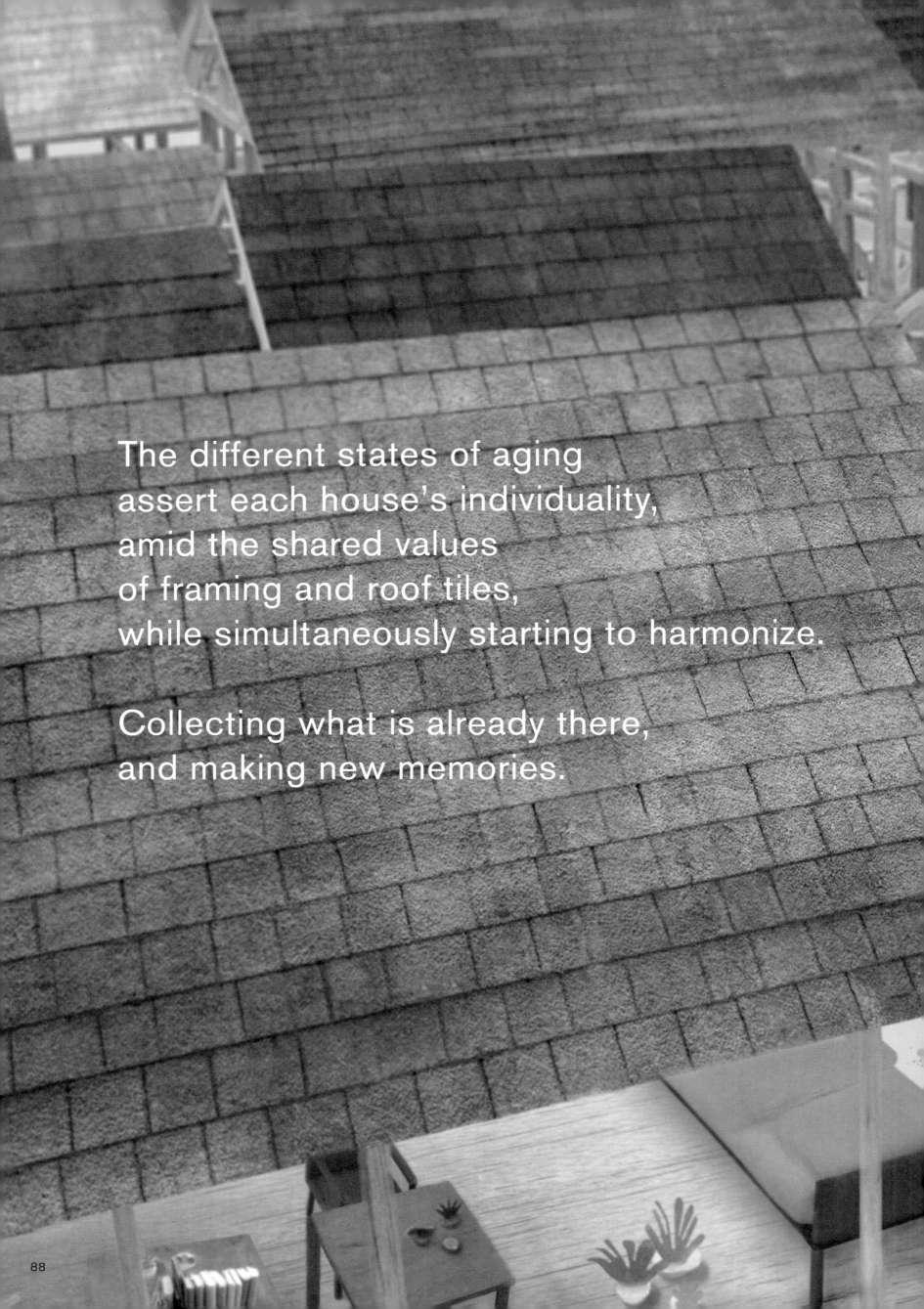

The different states of aging
assert each house's individuality,
amid the shared values
of framing and roof tiles,
while simultaneously starting to harmonize.

Collecting what is already there,
and making new memories.

Home for the Elderly   89

Thinking about architecture
can mean discovering
new realms unknown to us,
and expanding our everyday world.

Renovations on an old building:
a brick structure
of around 40,000 square meters,
built in the nineteenth century,
used as a museum.

Various investigations were carried out.
Above ground, the building was found
to be in excellent condition.
The space could likely be restored
to its original state.

Below ground, things were rather more dire.

Water was coming through in places,
bricks had crumbled to dust.

There were people squatting there illegally.

The plan: to take this dubious
subterranean space
no one was aware of, clean it up,
and bring it beautifully to the fore,
transforming the building.

Polytechnic Museum 95

Floor plan
of the existing basement.

Underneath, the building
is a maze of thick brick walls.
This will be turned into a large,
open entrance space.

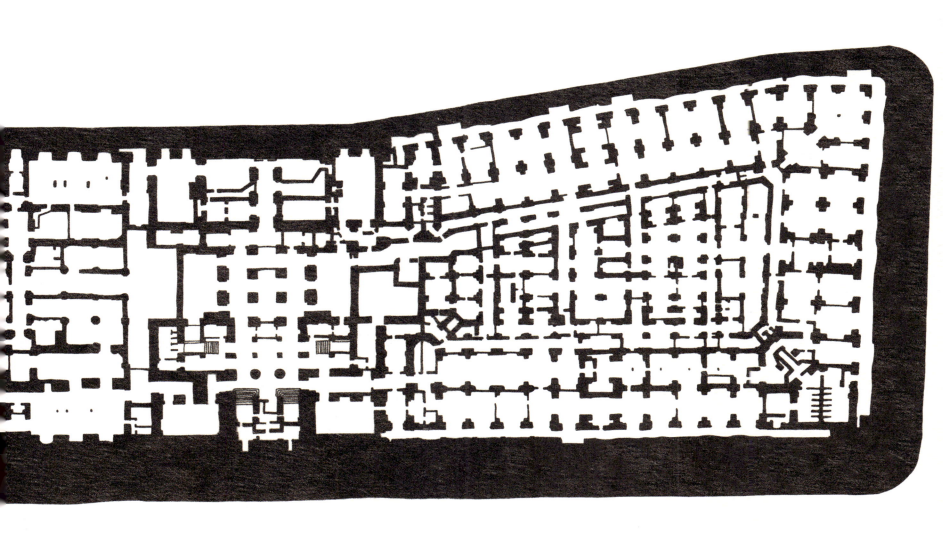

The original elevation.

The attractive facade
will be left untouched,
and by digging out
the perimeter of the building
in a gently sloping bowl,
what was the basement
will be turned into
a new above-ground level.

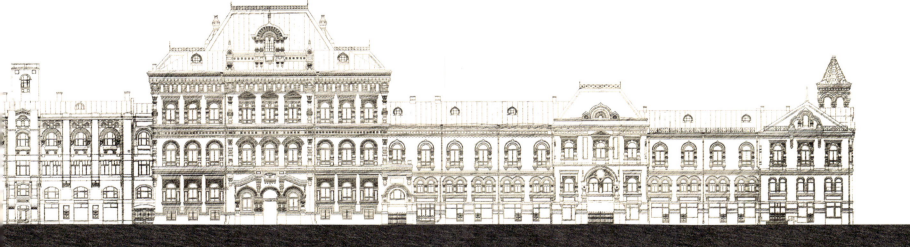

Polytechnic Museum

What was originally
the basement
will connect gently
to the surrounding ground,
forming a new ground level.

The above-ground section
of the building thus drops a level,
dramatically altering the proportions
of the facade as well,
giving the building
a totally different look.

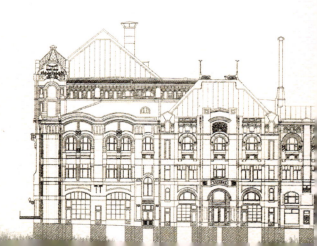

Removing the existing brick walls
reveals a cavernous pillared area.
A new, spacious entrance
emerges on the new ground level.

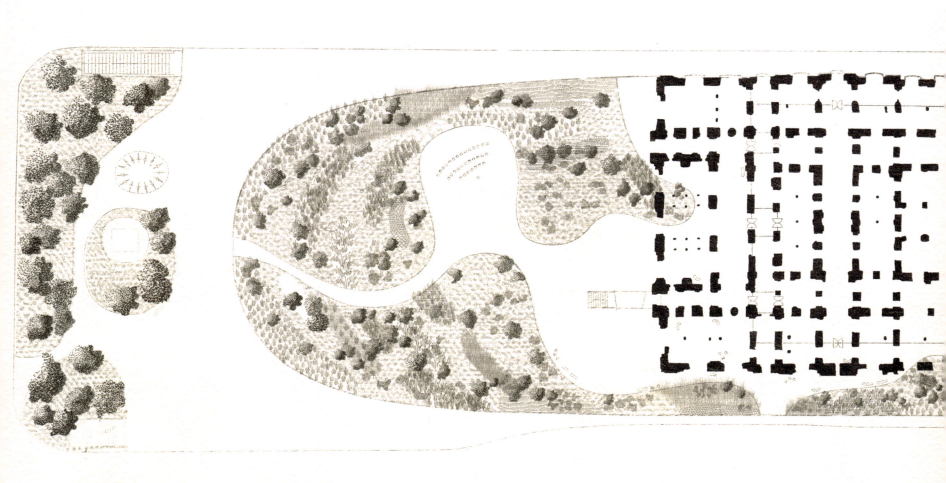

The bowl-shaped slope
becomes a lovely park.

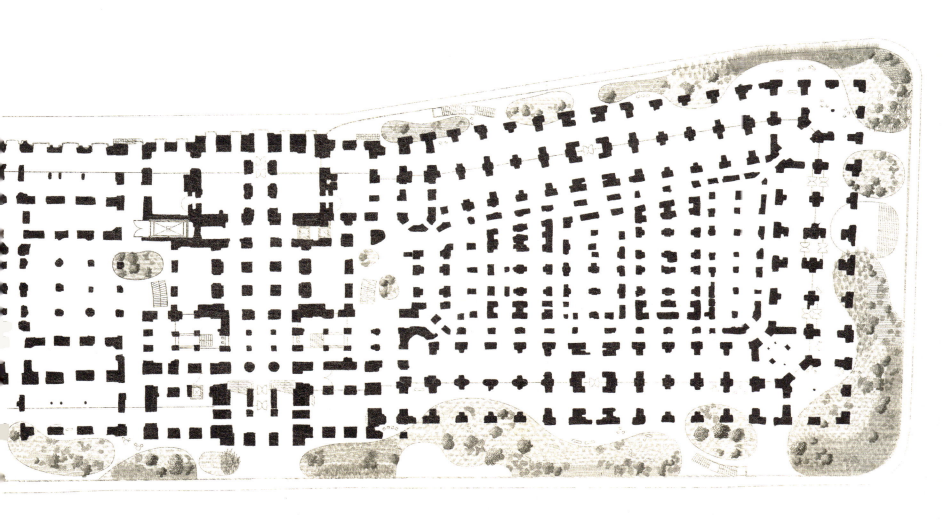

Polytechnic Museum

The surrounding ground
is dug out,
and the subterranean facade,
under the soil all this time,
shows itself above ground
for the first time.

With the walls gone,
the space opens out.
The pillars are reinforced.

Polytechnic Museum

Thus a space that
was there all the time
is rediscovered.

Nothing is added to
the old building.

It takes on
a new lease of life.

On some remote level,
architecture and
archeology are connected.

A stunningly beautiful location.
In a few years, it will be a resort.
This scene will no longer
exist as it is now.

A place very famous for stone.
The abundance of massive rocks
forms a striking landscape.
Eight weekend residences
are planned for here.
The disappearing landscape
will be preserved inside the building.

A survey of the large rocks
is carried out on the site.

With just a few adjustments
to the original arrangement
of the rocks,
new living spaces are found.

8 Villas in Dali

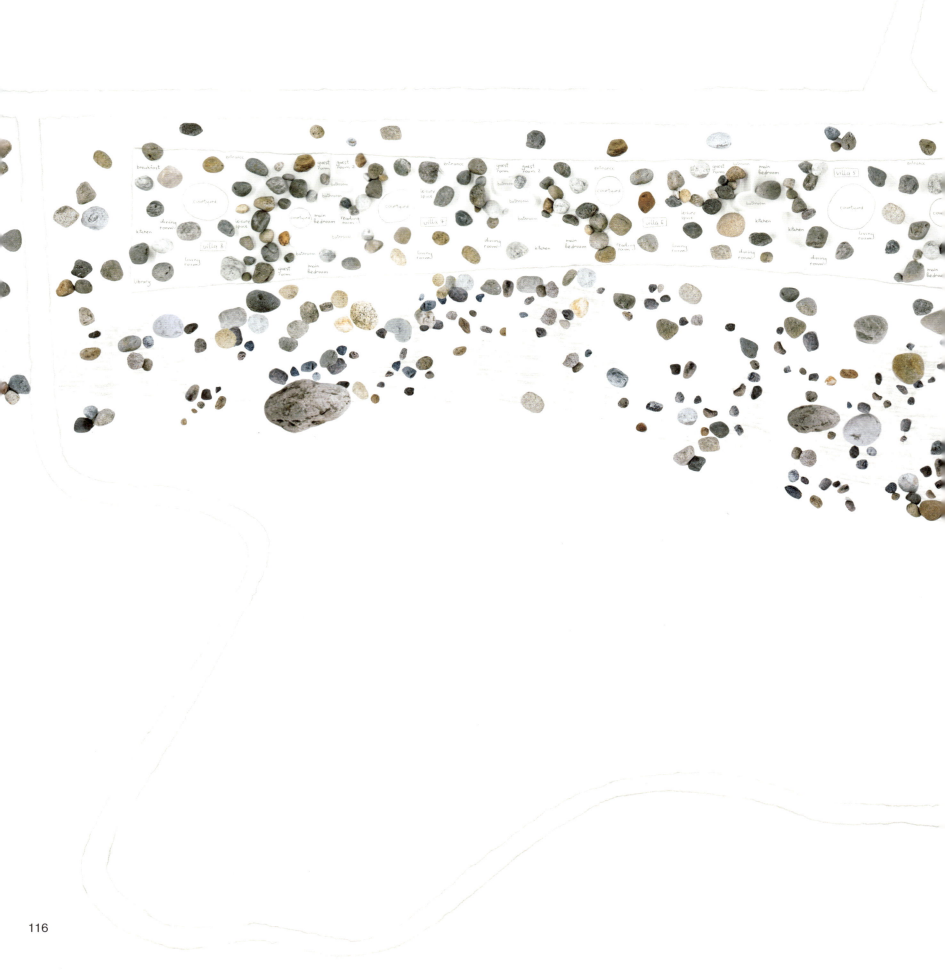

Walking the site, physically sensing
small places amid the vast field of boulders,
manageable, livable spaces are found.

These are joined to form
a single large structure.

Each boulder serves as a pillar, combining to support one large, 300-meter-long roof.

8 Villas in Dali 119

As the environs change rapidly, the landscape here will be preserved inside the building, integrated with the panorama of rocks on the river flats. It will remain part of the lives of those who reside here.

8 Villas in Dali

The large rocks in the house,
remaining as part of the landscape,
look even larger than
when seen outdoors.

Like a site that looked very small
before a house is built on the land,
feeling much larger once
the house is finished,
and you are inside.

8 Villas in Dali 123

Simply by working out in detail
the physical dimensions of the space,
and its size in terms
of bodily sensation,
a new environment can be produced
without altering anything
in the existing one.

8 Villas in Dali   125

Looking at it on a child's scale and from a child's perspective, architecture as we know it is fundamentally altered, because architecture is based on adult scale.

To a child, a table is architecture.

Kids Park

Thinking about a space for children.

First, forget any ideas of scale, values,
the usual architectural viewpoints.
Try imagining as spaces things
we don't usually think of as spaces.

For example,
if time all around us
came almost to a standstill,
if we were as small as tiny elves,
to us, animals would probably
be huge landscapes.

Think about making
a children's playground.
For example,
a dog for a big roof.
A bear for a dome.
A hippo for a cave.

Kids Park 131

Scenes of animals appear, one after another.

Kids Park

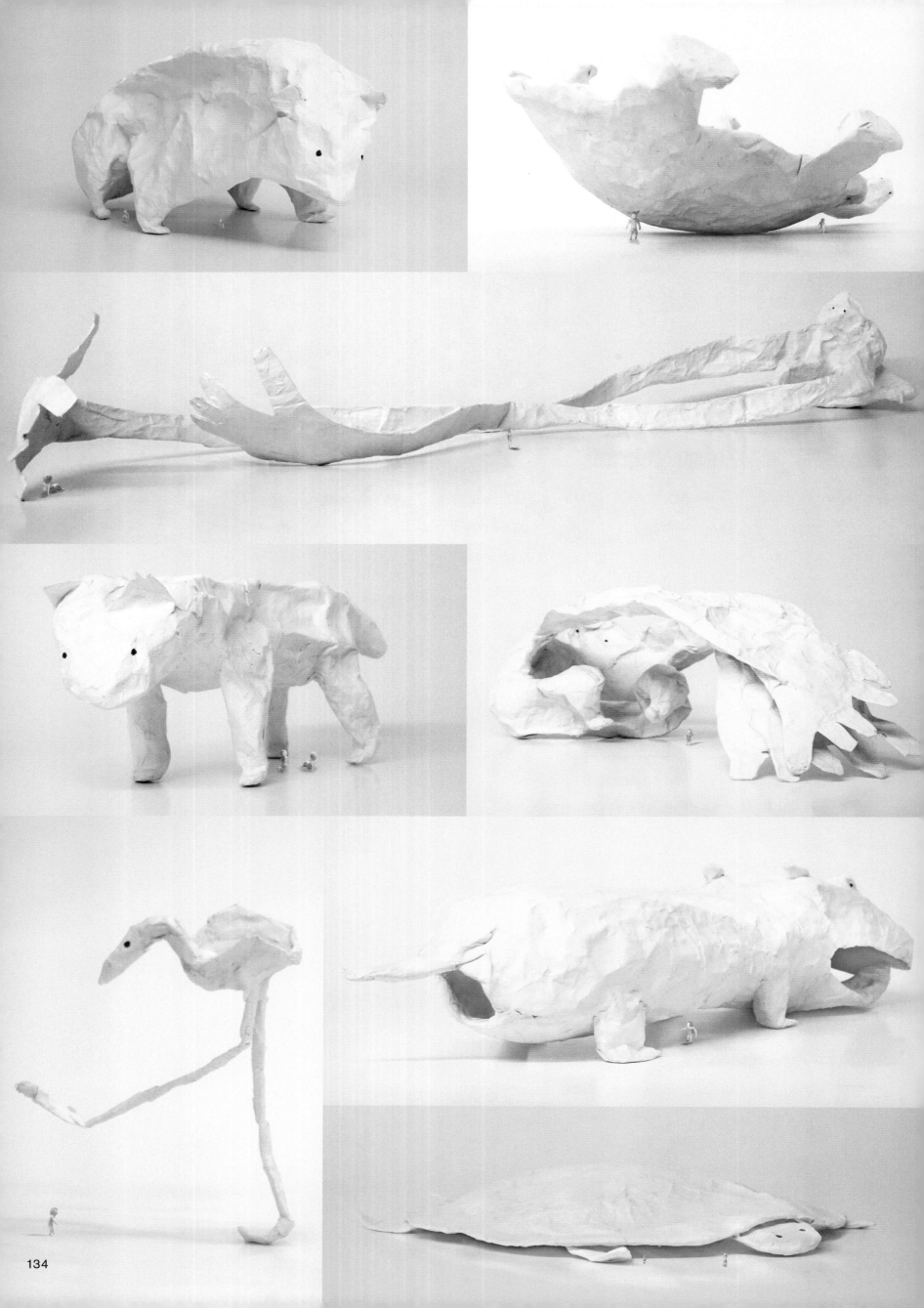

The animals are architecture.

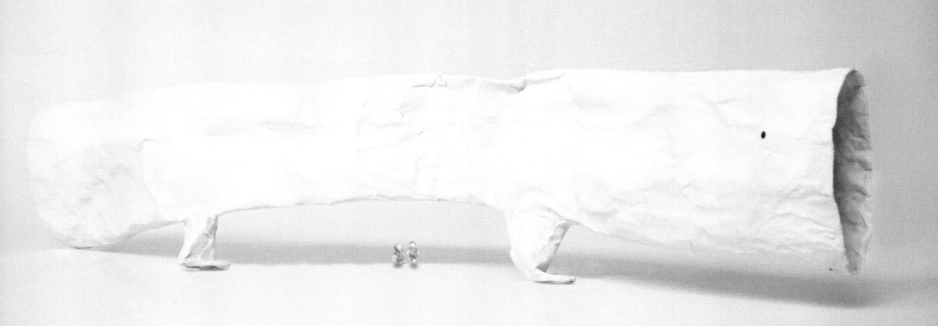

Kids Park

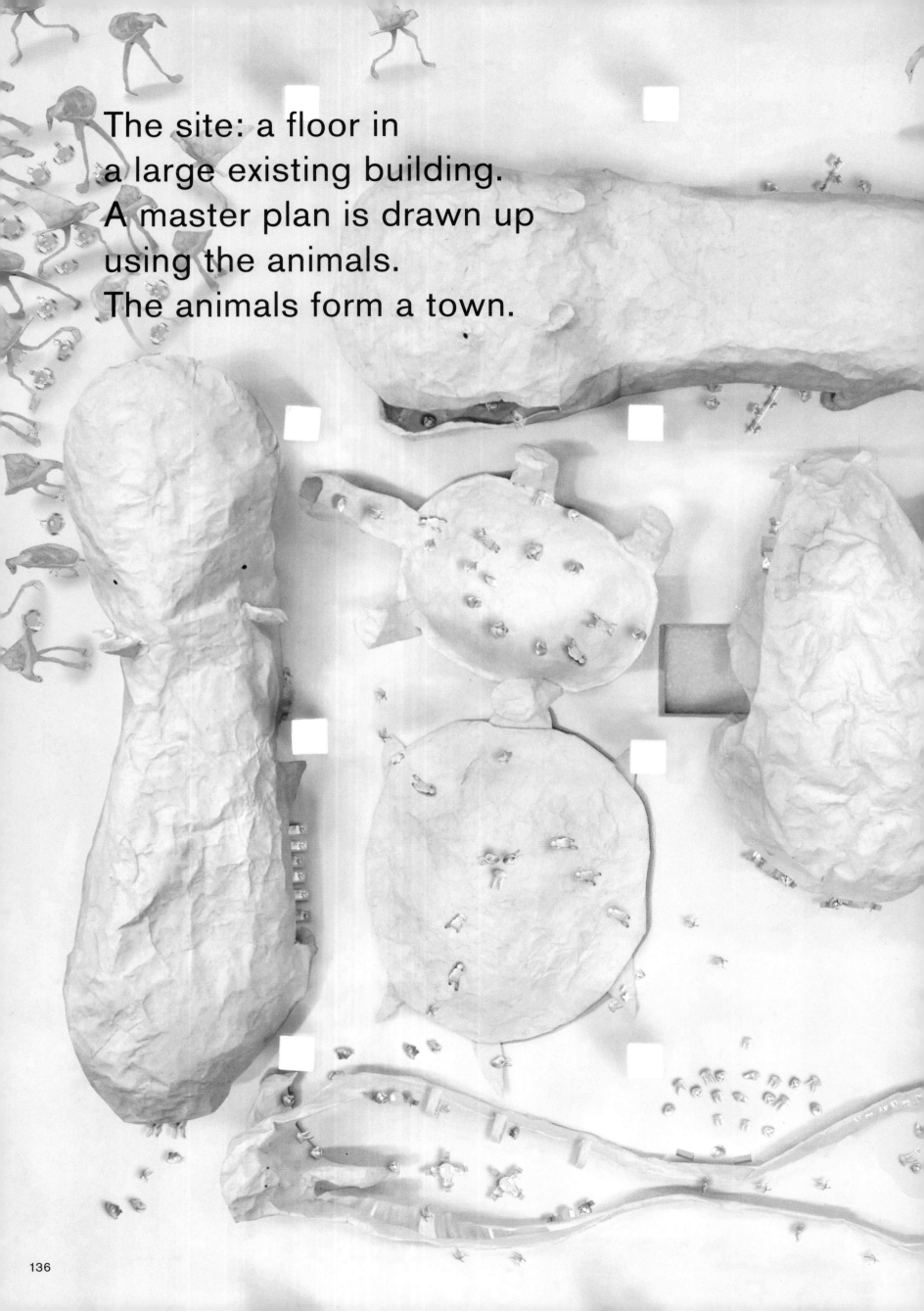

The site: a floor in a large existing building. A master plan is drawn up using the animals. The animals form a town.

When the world is viewed from a child's perspective, animals, plants, rocks, mountains, clouds, buildings, all form equal parts of the scenery.

Kids Park

Thinking about architecture
means imagining the world
in ways beyond scale.

Architectural structures
are much bigger than people.
We use models and drawings
of various scales
to obtain an overall picture.
Seeing spaces within these.

Children's ideas,
and the ideas of architecture,
share a great deal.

Both look at the world
in ways beyond scale.

Cloud Garden   139

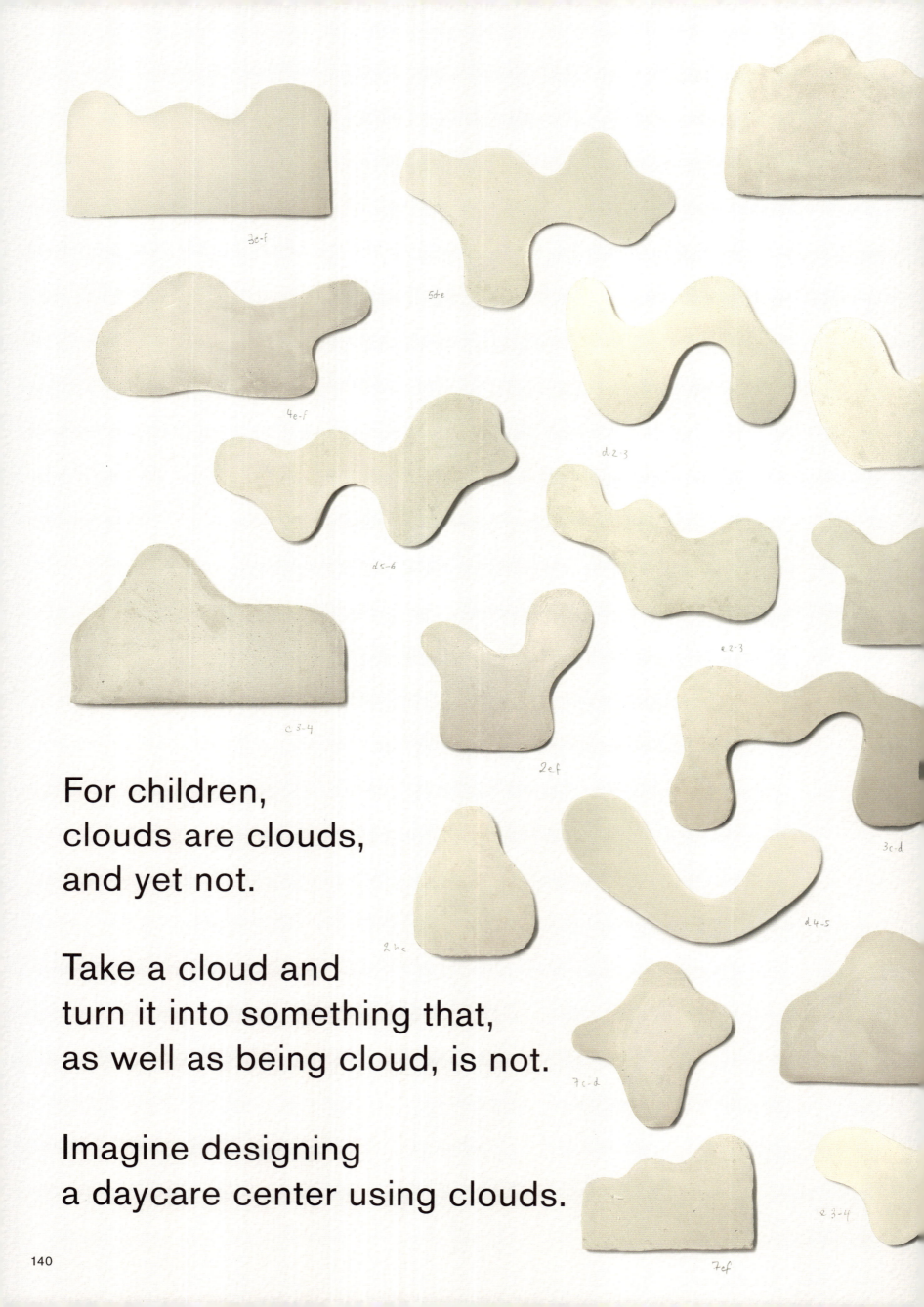

For children,
clouds are clouds,
and yet not.

Take a cloud and
turn it into something that,
as well as being cloud, is not.

Imagine designing
a daycare center using clouds.

Cloud Garden 141

Gazing at clouds,
imagine a mountain and stand on top,
gazing at clouds,
think of bread and feel hungry,
gazing at clouds,
be reminded of monsters and feel scared,
gazing at clouds,
sense a whale, climb on it and feel happy.

Among endless imaginings,
spaces of all sorts emerge.

Cloud Garden

Think about architecture
as it fits into a child's world,
where dreams and reality overlap.
Think about designing a kindergarten.

In a world before subjectivity and objectivity,
immanence and transcendence,
concrete and abstract, diverge.
This is the study for the initial plan.

Forest Kindergarten

A crocodile taking a flower in its claw,
a whale and a stag beetle,
sitting amiably together.
An octopus using its many arms
to shake hands with everyone.

In the whole, linked in such ways,
the independence of each is diluted.
Turning it into one large, fuzzy, hazy mass.
Develop the study a little further.

Forest Kindergarten

Lots of different play overlaps, to avoid connecting place and experience one to one. So that countless, conflicting experiences pile one upon another.

Designed, and undesigned
are viewed as of similar value.
All different scales: that of small children,
that of adults, are personal in scale.

Think of architecture like that.

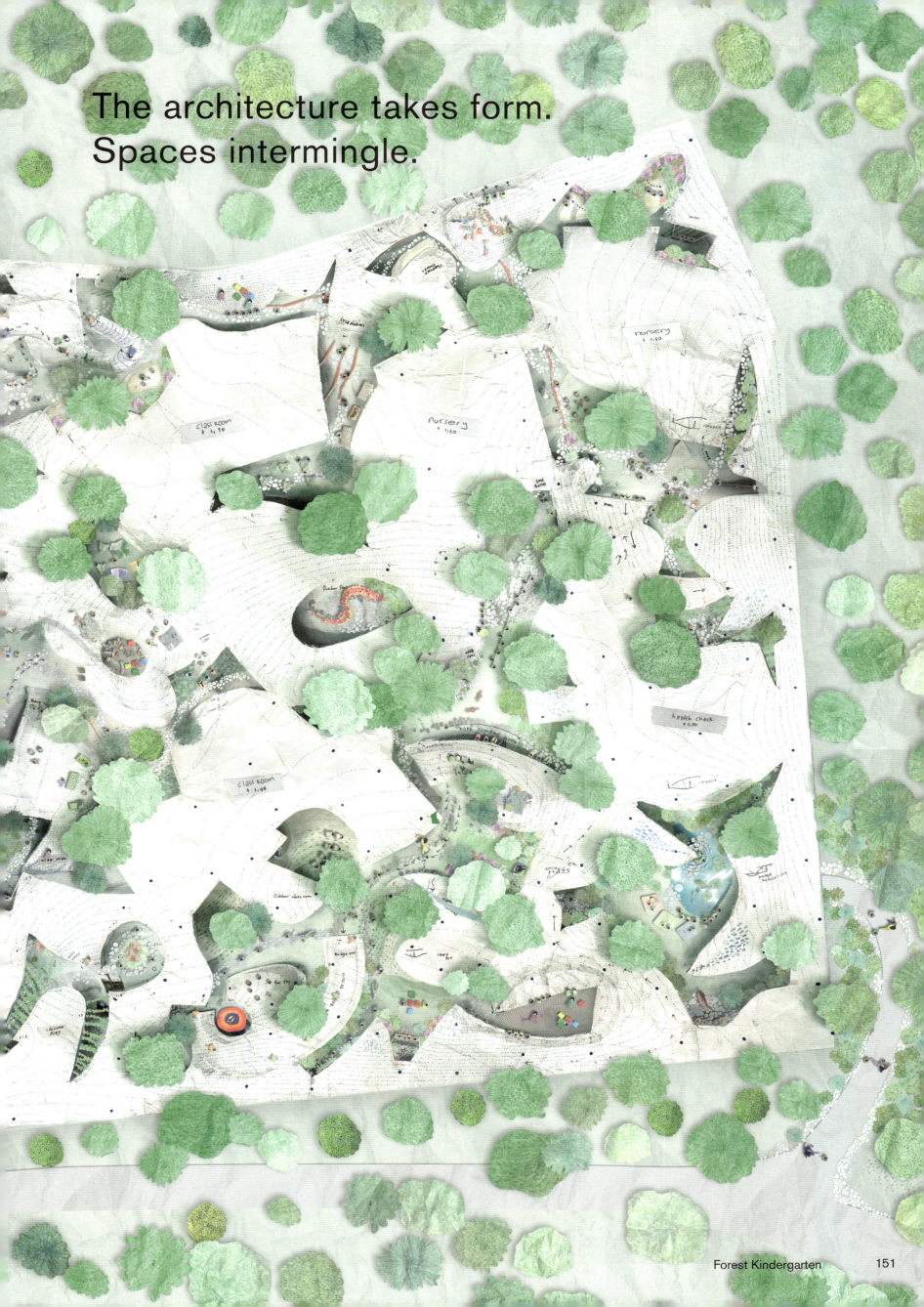

The architecture takes form.
Spaces intermingle.

Forest Kindergarten

Some places are enclosed in glass, making classrooms.
Some places are open to the sky, making gardens.

Forest Kindergarten

In some places,
the architecture spans the children's world,
adults becoming giants.

Forest Kindergarten

Adult-scale, child-scale, interior, exterior, play equipment, landscape, plants, structures, brightness, darkness, quiet, noise, architecture extends amid all kinds of things merging into each other.

Forest Kindergarten

Sketch lots of plans.
Study the sketches over and over.

Ponder them at length in different ways,
envisioning spaces within the lines.
Like finding clearings in the jungle.

Forest Kindergarten

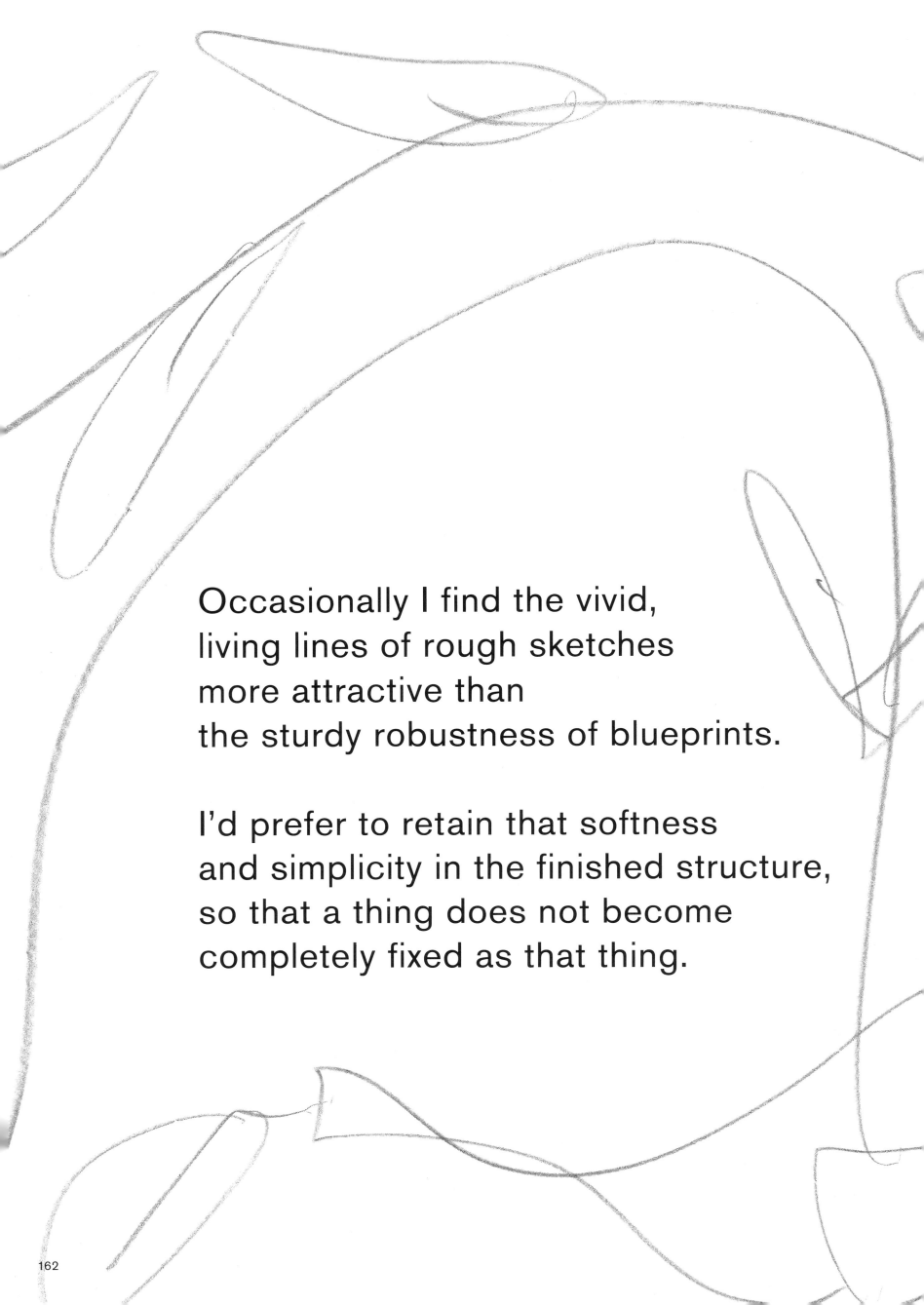

Occasionally I find the vivid,
living lines of rough sketches
more attractive than
the sturdy robustness of blueprints.

I'd prefer to retain that softness
and simplicity in the finished structure,
so that a thing does not become
completely fixed as that thing.

Cloud Arch   163

Imagine building a huge 60-meter gate
in the middle of town,
spanning the road,
like a cloud sketched in mid-air.

Cloud Arch

Cloud Arch

Something to gaze on absentmindedly.

Cloud Arch

A place for people to come together.
The place to meet.
Lodged somewhere
in everyone's memory.

Cloud Arch

At the same time,
that would seem
a different shape
to everyone who sees it.

Cloud Arch

I imagined making
such a gate in
the middle of town.

Cloud Arch

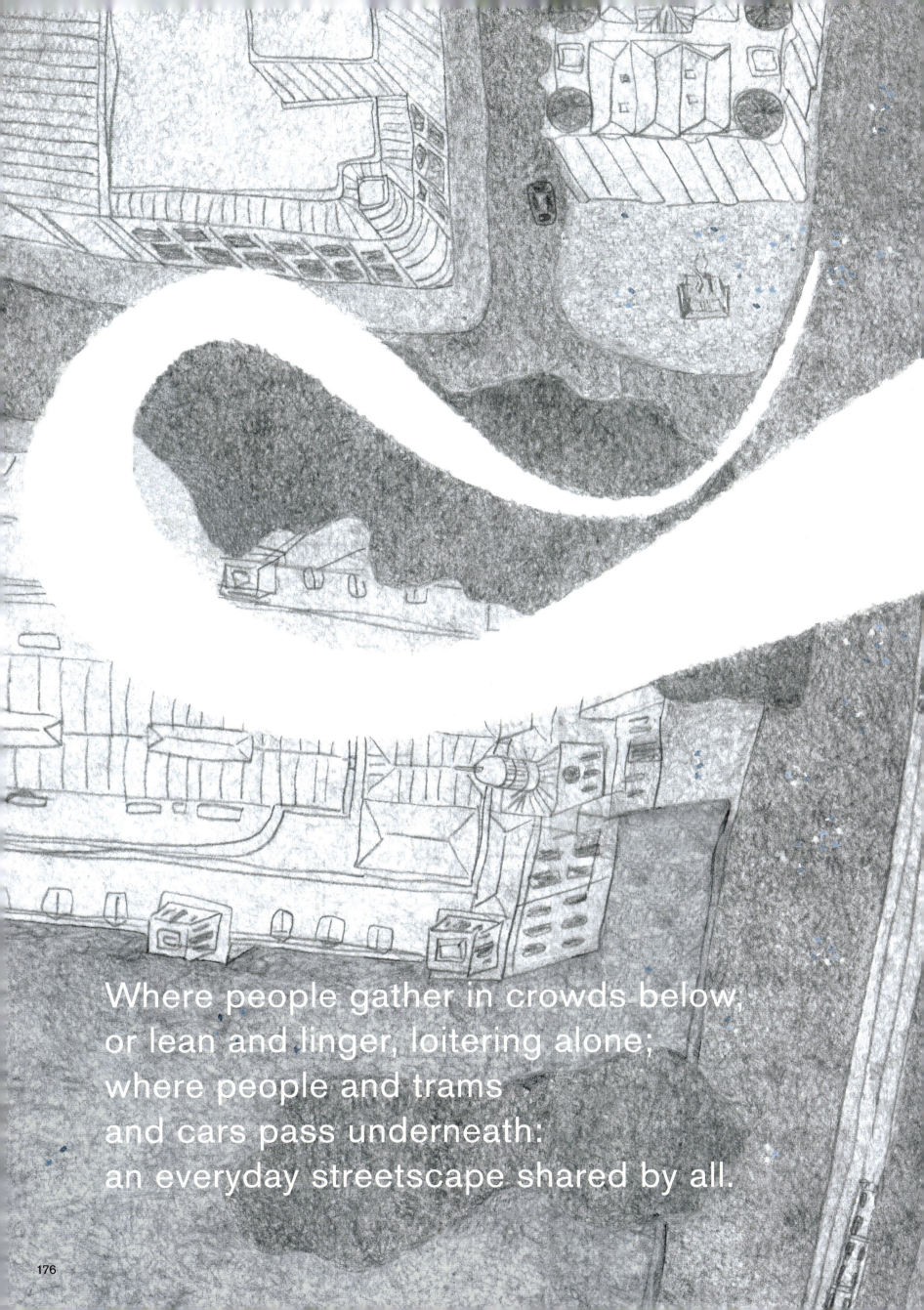

Where people gather in crowds below,
or lean and linger, loitering alone;
where people and trams
and cars pass underneath:
an everyday streetscape shared by all.

Cloud Arch 177

Just like a cloud,
changing into different things.
Able to coexist with
what was there before,
and also get along well with
whatever turns up.
Flexible, fuzzy plans
like this fascinate me.

Cloud Arch

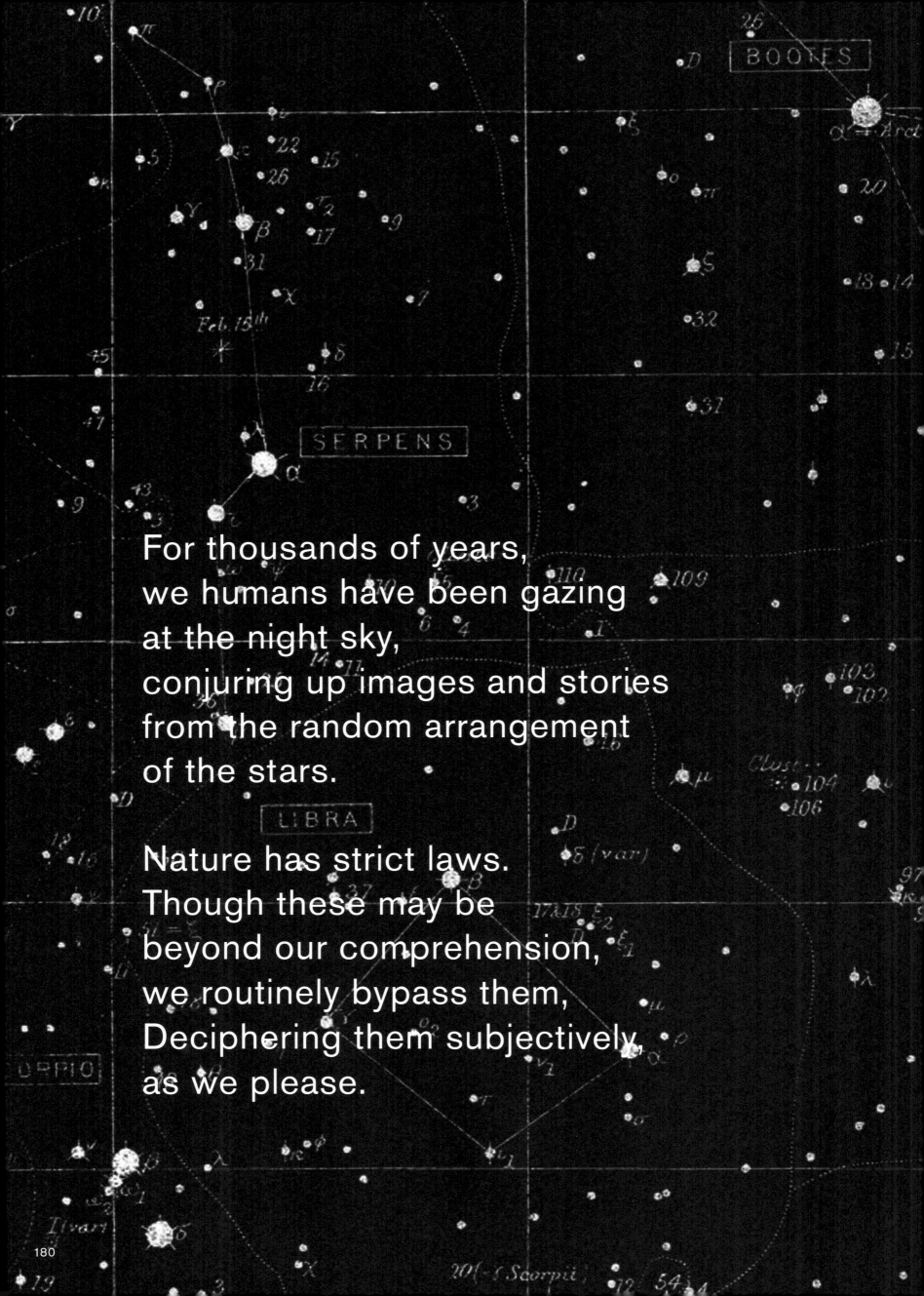

For thousands of years,
we humans have been gazing
at the night sky,
conjuring up images and stories
from the random arrangement
of the stars.

Nature has strict laws.
Though these may be
beyond our comprehension,
we routinely bypass them,
Deciphering them subjectively,
as we please.

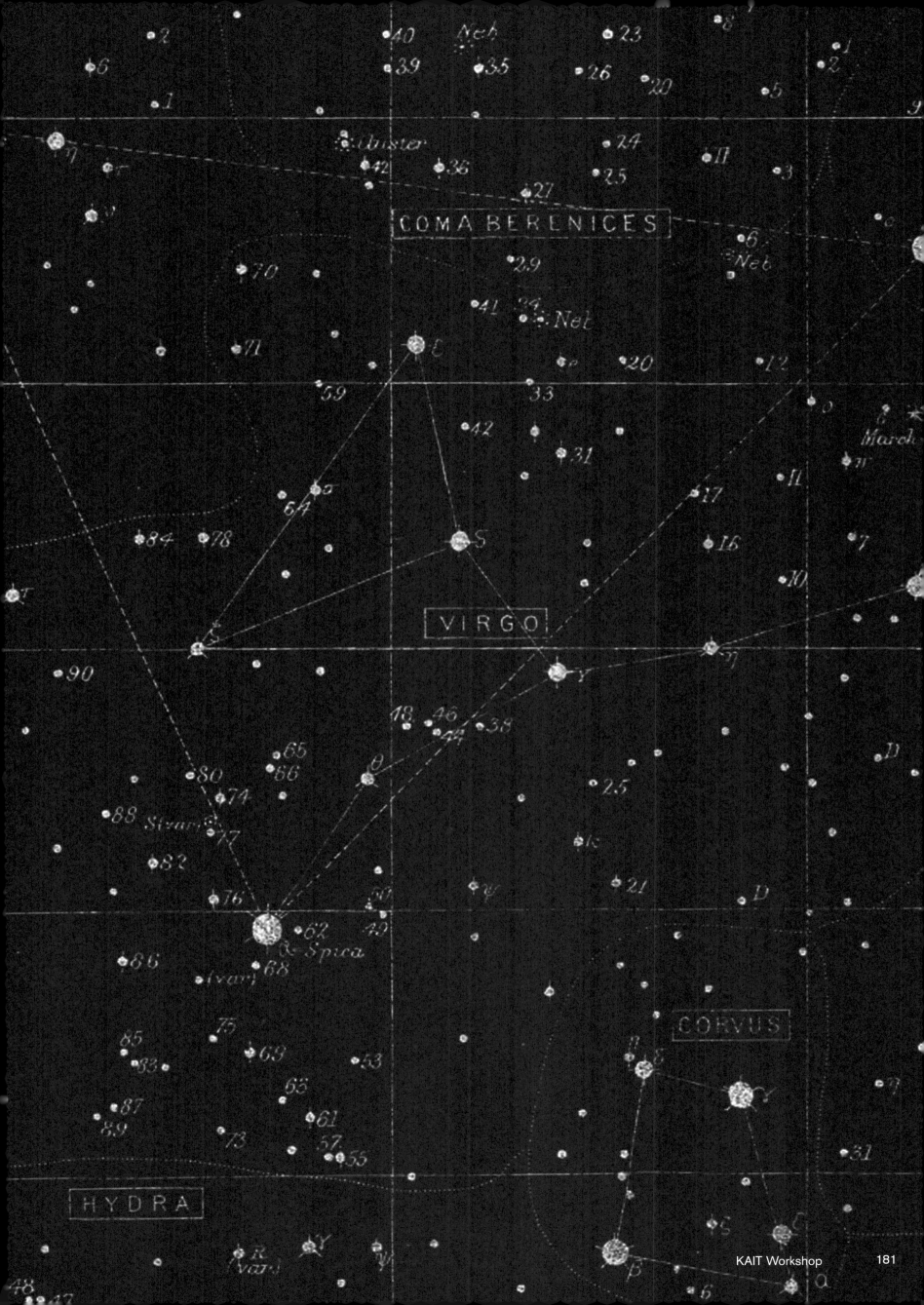

Can architecture be freed
in the same manner?

Given the freedom,
despite being rigorous
in its intended use,
and planned accordingly,
to transcend this
and view space subjectively,
enabling different uses.
A freedom open
to multiple interpretations.

machine tool space

shop

counter

KAIT Workshop

A workshop for students.

This building has no walls.
All structures are supported
solely by pillars.
All the pillars have different proportions,
are oriented in different ways,
positioned at different intervals.

KAIT Workshop

Each pillar is decided
individually, meticulously.
At the same time,
a meticulous plan
is rendered transparent.

Planning while making
the plan's intent
no longer visible,
becomes the intent
of this plan.

KAIT Workshop

188

Random arrangement.
A ground plan of trees in a forest.
The arrangement of stars
also resembles that of trees in a forest.
That we sense a shared randomness
in these two things
that appear unrelated
may be due to that randomness
belonging to the essence of nature.

Our everyday lies between
the manifestation
of carefully calculated results,
and free interpretation.

KAIT Workshop 191

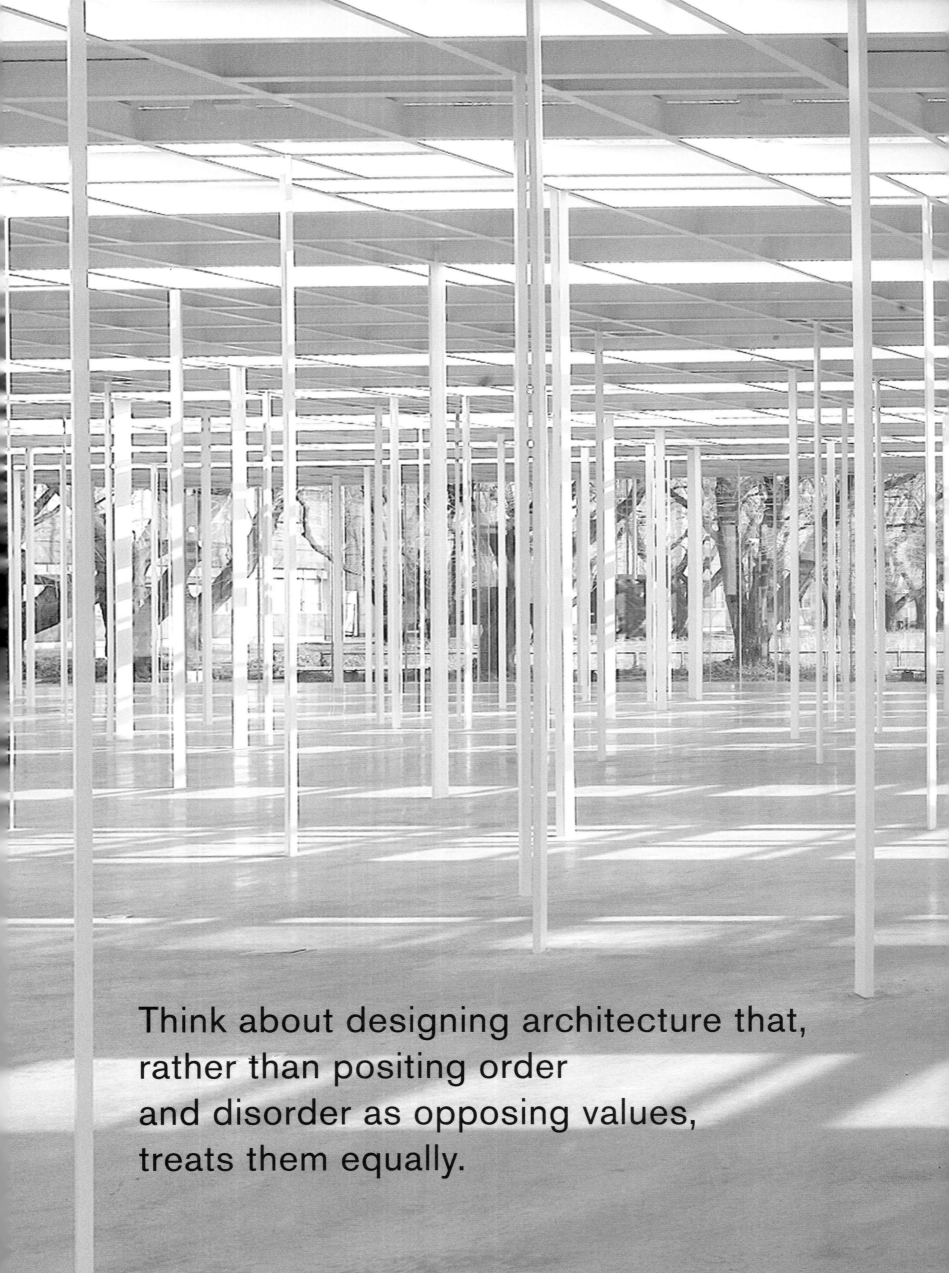

Think about designing architecture that, rather than positing order
and disorder as opposing values,
treats them equally.

KAIT Workshop

Discover spaces freely,
assigning them a function each time.

Whenever a piece of
architecture is completed,
it is revealed to be attractive
in all sorts of ways
over and above the architect's intent.
Perhaps it then makes sense
when thinking about architecture,
to be more conscious of this
from the planning stage.

KAIT Workshop

The idea: to build something
that nimbly transcends
the architect's intent.

Incorporating the unpredictable
fluctuations and oscillations of
nature in architecture.

Thinking not of a homogeneous,
machine-made sort of comfort,
but a comfort suited
to the location, each time.

A facility for the contemplation of
world peace.
Situated on the sea in a northern land.
The idea is to create a new outside,
inside the structure.

For meditating on peace,
while rocking gently in a little boat.

House of Peace   199

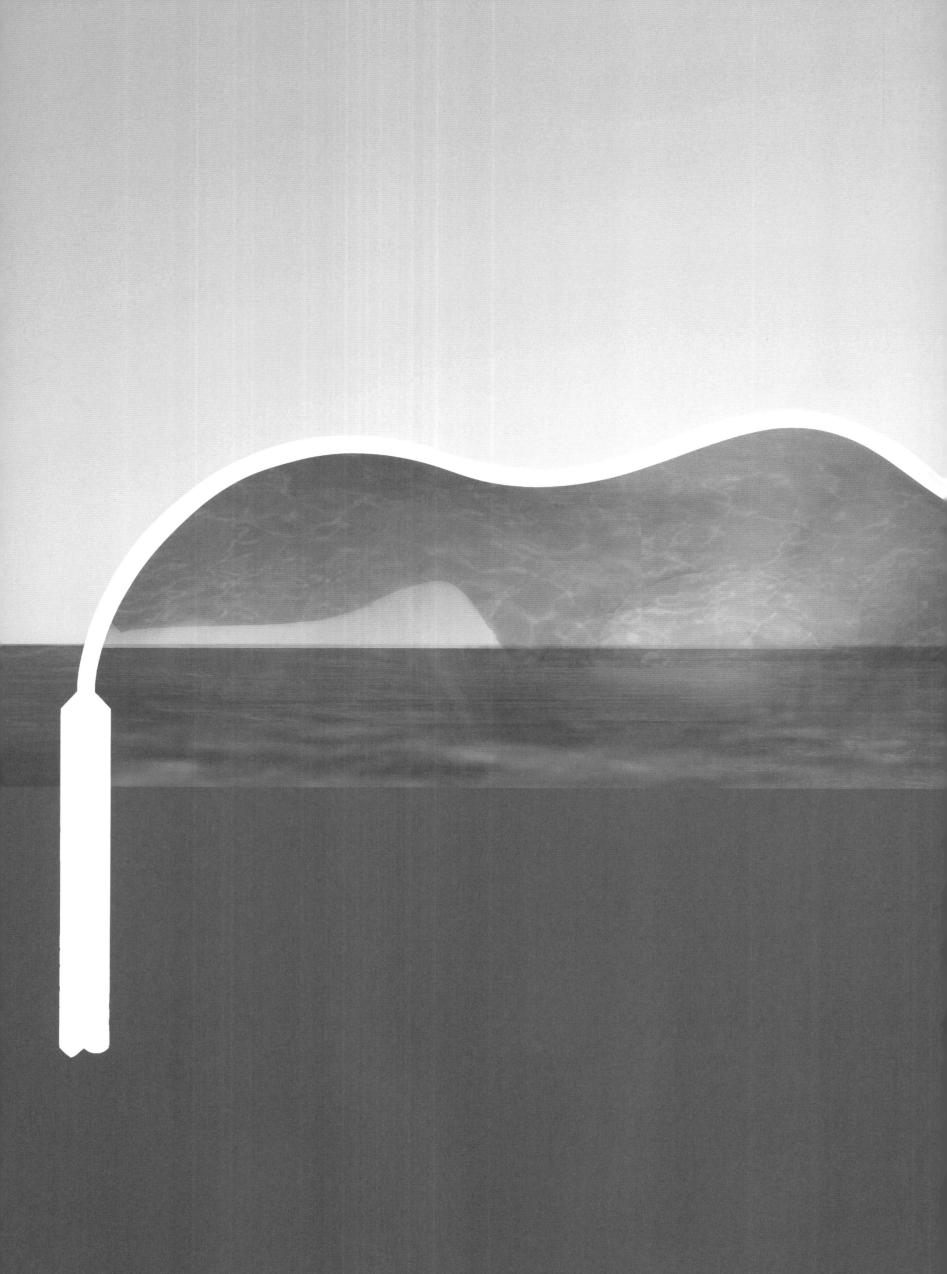

A cloud-like construction.
Supported by piles,
standing in the ocean,
as if floating upon it.

House of Peace

Designed so that
the shell-shaped construction
and the glass
in the opening
sink into the water.

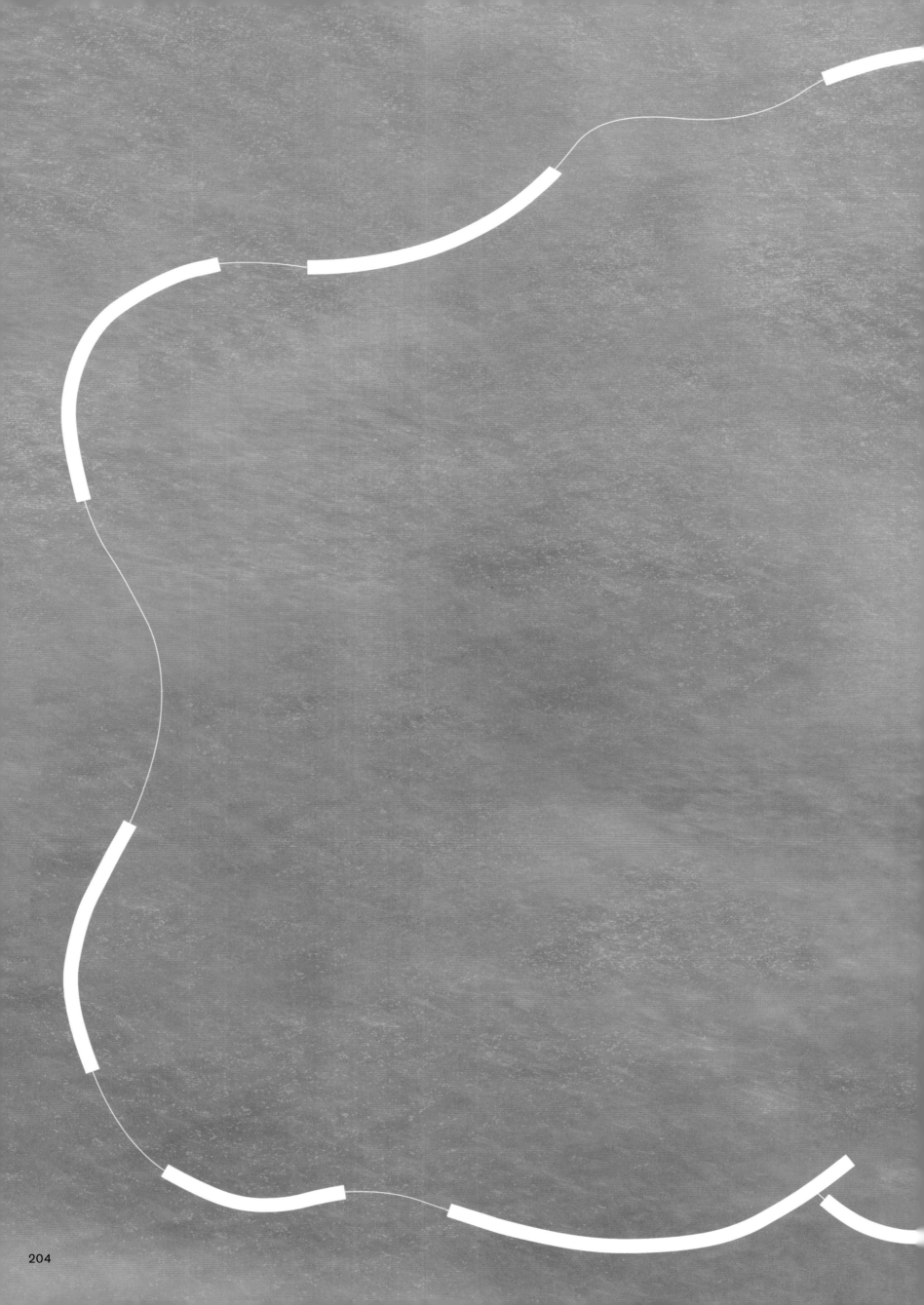

Seawater penetrates the interior.
Simultaneously separated
from the surrounding currents,
settling there tranquilly.

From summer to autumn,
light from the sun slowly warms
the seawater inside.
In winter, the well-heated seawater
gently warms the interior.

In summer,
the structure is opened up,
allowing refreshing breezes
and ripples to flow inside.

The openings are low,
lots of light reflecting off
the shallow seafloor,
and inside, permeating up
through the water's surface.

The light changes
the surface of the water,
the space,
according to the time of
day and season.

House of Peace

Inside, the structure is devoid
of mechanical devices.
In winter people feel warm seawater,
in summer, breezes skating
across the water's surface.
From the water, light seeping out,
reflected off the seafloor.

Creating a landscape inside architecture.
Creating nature inside architecture.

Creating nature
that can coexist with humans.
Applying different values
from different angles
in approaching nature.

Natural rocks.
Architecture like a rock.
One of the client's few requirements was
"to design the most solid
piece of architecture possible."

The brief was to design a restaurant
and housing for the owner.

"A building that will acquire
added weight over time.
Nothing light, such as prefabricated
or steel-frame construction.
Nothing too slick or glossy;
a building with more of
the rough edges of nature.
Authentic cooking requires
that sort of space."

Clouds, mountains, trees, and rocks
are all made naturally.
Myriad phenomena overlap,
manifesting in complex forms.

There is no evenness in nature.
No two things are the same.
Consider the allure of that kind of diversity.

Dig holes in the ground.

House & Restaurant   215

Pour in concrete.

House & Restaurant

Dig out the concrete masses.
A structure appears.

House & Restaurant

A roof forms in the earth.

House & Restaurant

Walls form in the earth.

Dig,
and spaces emerge
between the masses.

Some places become the house,
some the restaurant.

RESTAURANT
KITCHEN

BAR

RESTAURANT
ENTRANCE

COURTYARD

WC

COURTYARD

BATHROOM

BEDROOM

HOUSE
ENTRANCE

House & Restaurant

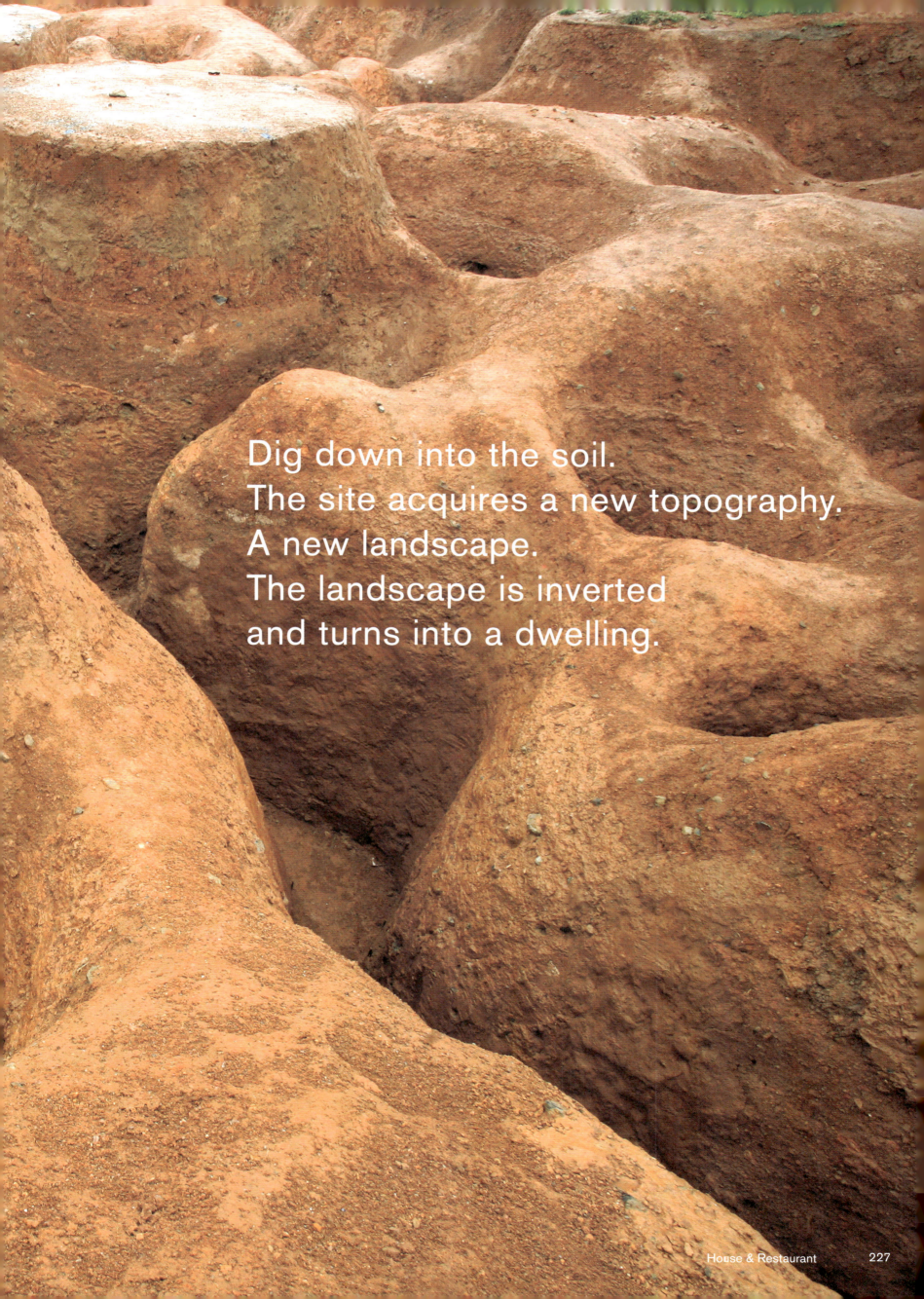

Dig down into the soil.
The site acquires a new topography.
A new landscape.
The landscape is inverted
and turns into a dwelling.

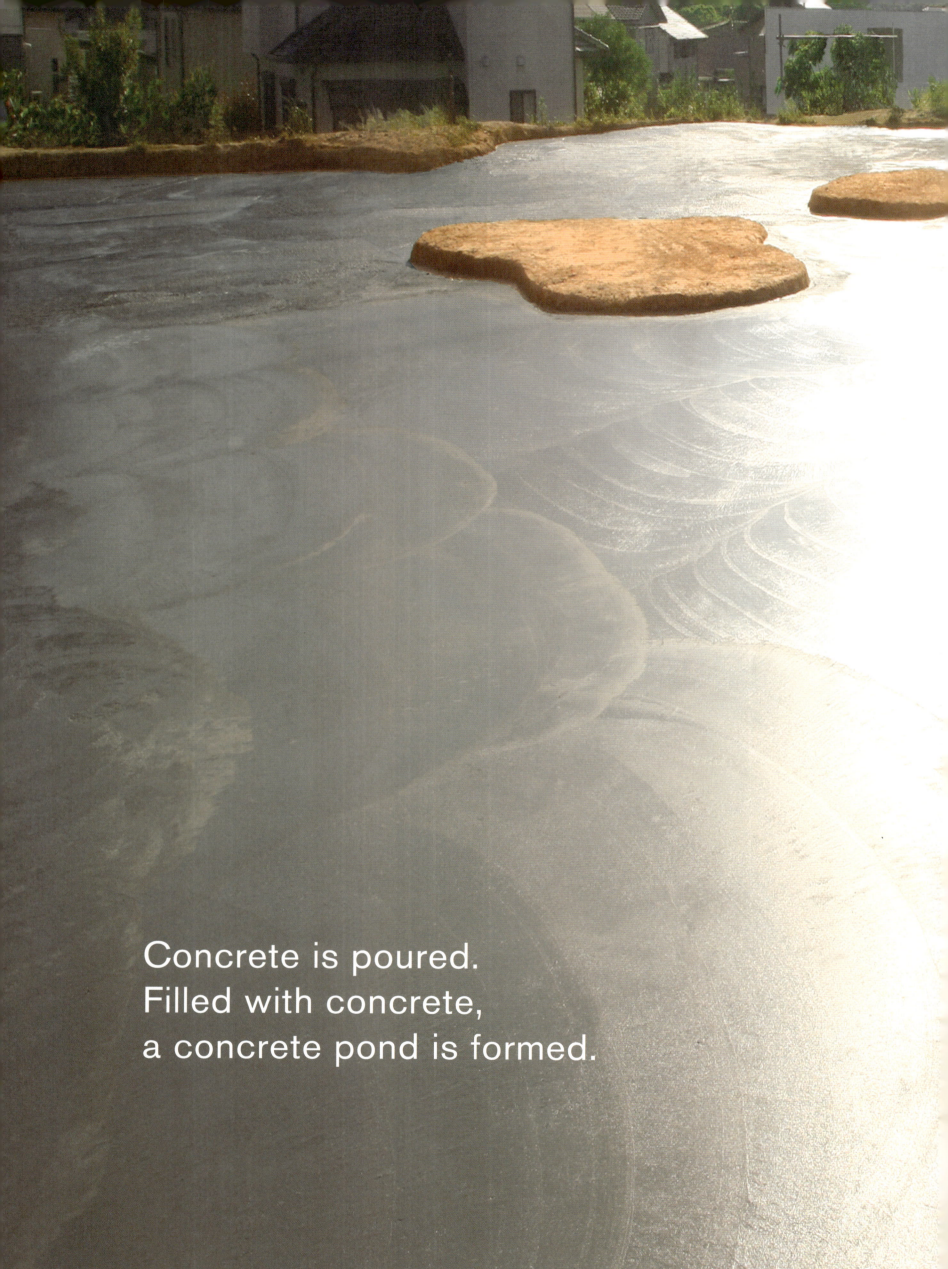

Concrete is poured.
Filled with concrete,
a concrete pond is formed.

House & Restaurant

Dig into the earth,
and spaces are revealed.

House & Restaurant

Soil clinging to the concrete
becomes part of the finish.
A technique for repairing
crumbling earthen walls
is used to fix the earth in place.

Soil strata remain intact.
The uneven state of the ground
gives the space its texture.
Glass is fitted to form the interior.

House & Restaurant

The spaces formed by the voids
are inverted, becoming volumes.
The soil volumes are inverted
to become spaces.
One place forms the kitchen.
Another is seating for diners.
Another a living room.
Another the bedroom.
A place is made for each,
becoming a restaurant
and a home.

Spaces the architect intended,
and those unintended, merge.

For some reason, food tastes better
when consumed in motley eateries
in shabby old backstreets
than in bland restaurants
situated on a floor
of a shiny new office building.

The naturalness
of what was there originally;
the settled sense,
the distinctive atmosphere
of something there since forever.
Values such as these
are worked into the design.

House & Restaurant   239

Valley spaces have a mystery about them that transcends human knowledge. From where does that quality come?

Chapel of Valley 241

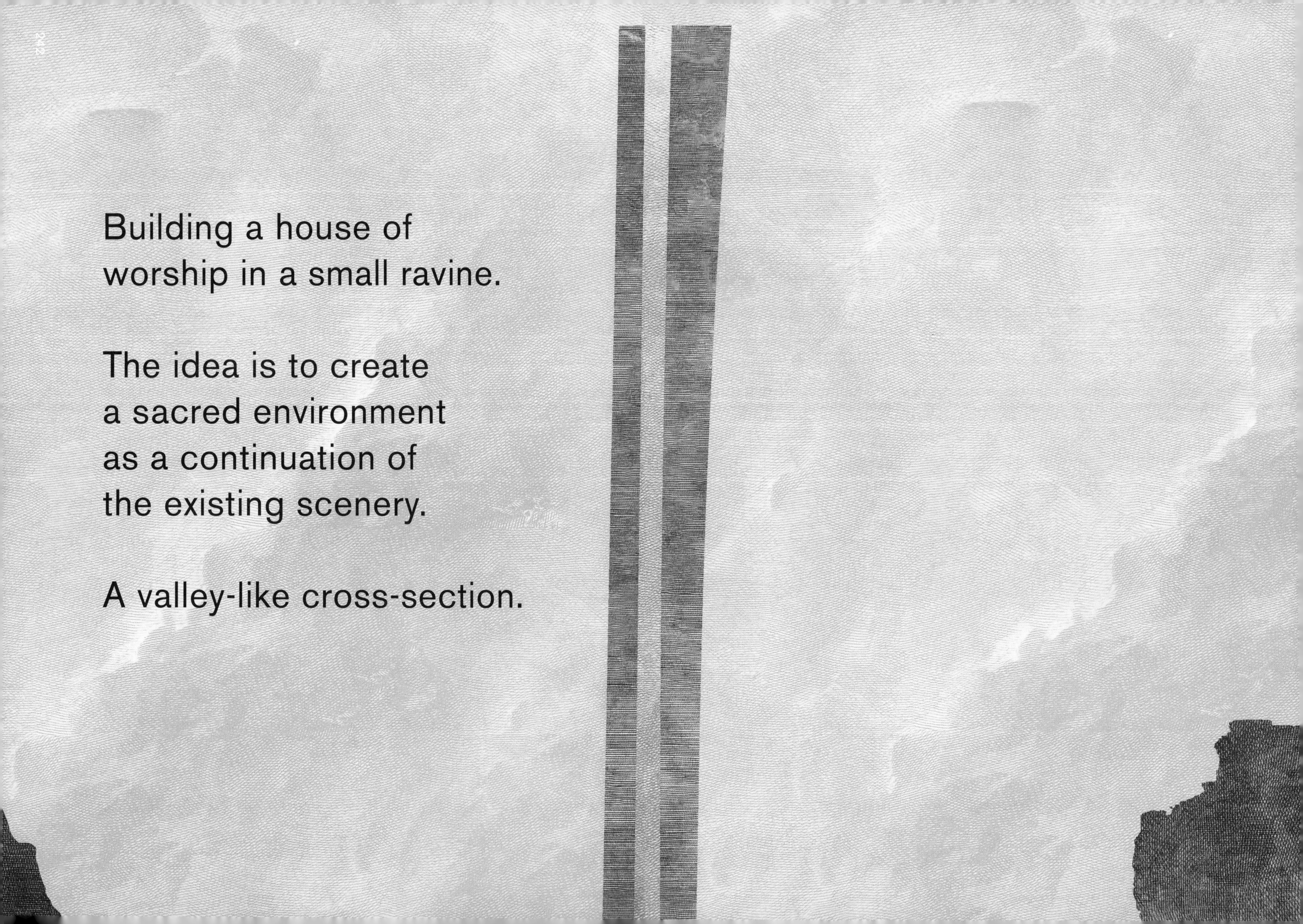

Building a house of
worship in a small ravine.

The idea is to create
a sacred environment
as a continuation of
the existing scenery.

A valley-like cross-section.

Chapel of Valley 243

The entrance is 1.3 meters wide, 45 meters tall.

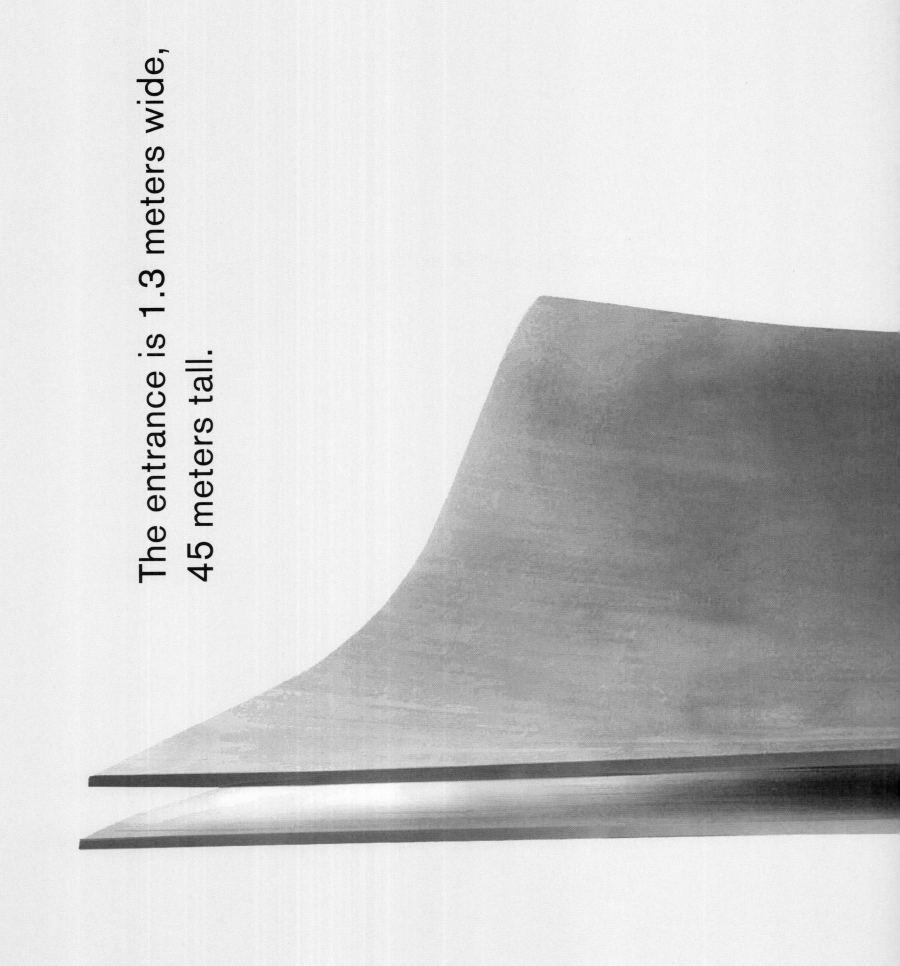

Chapel of Valley

Light enters from
45 meters above,
very little making it through.
The further in,
the wider and lighter
the space becomes.
Light radiates
from the depths of
the building.

Chapel of Valley

At the very back is the chapel.
Filled with light
descending right to the base.

Chapel of Valley   249

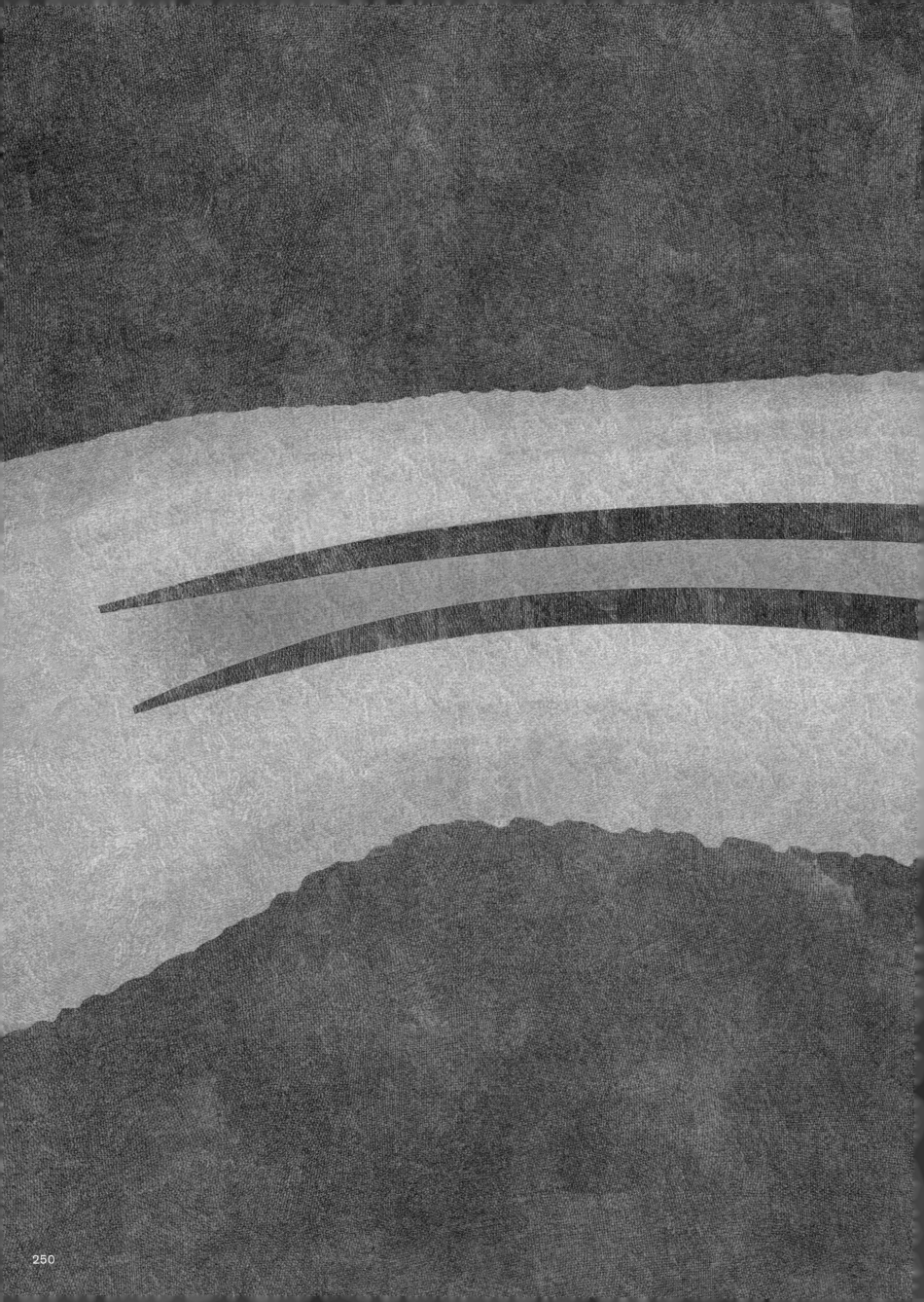

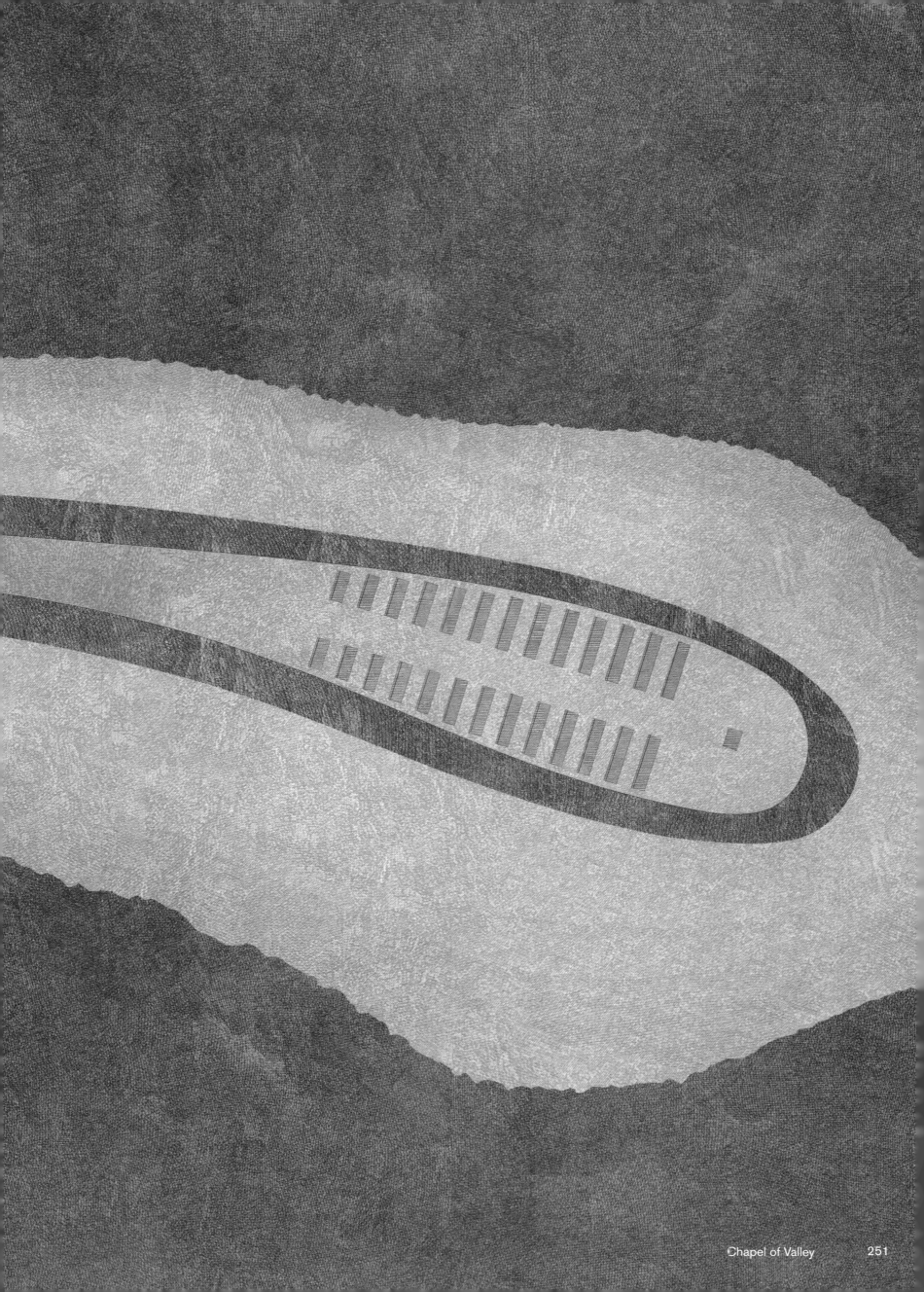

Chapel of Valley

Chapel in a valley.

Scenery has a shape.
Even the smallest gully
has the shape of a space.
The narrow, high space of a valley.

Think of a narrower, taller space.

A space more valley-like in quality
than the original valley.

A sacred valley emerges within the architecture.

The original valley and new valley connect in an understated fashion. A chapel filled with gentle light stands deep in a valley.

Chapel of Valley

254

Water is shapeless.
Water is poured
into a shallow valley-like landform
that extends endlessly,
passing along it,
flowing, forming a river.
The topography
giving the water shape,
forming the bones of
the scenery.

256

A site on a lake.
Think of architecture
on the same scale as the lake.

Cultural Center

Consider a very long building complex.
A structure one kilometer long,
spanning the lake.
Giving shape to the water
and forming scenery.

Cultural Center

Architecture gives the water shape,
pillars give the lake shape,
in the manner that topography as structure
gives shape to water, forming a river.

A new river appears in the lake.

A place for people is created
in the river, in the form of a sandbank.

Cultural Center   263

264

A one-kilometer-long structure
forms the framework for scenery.

Cultural Center

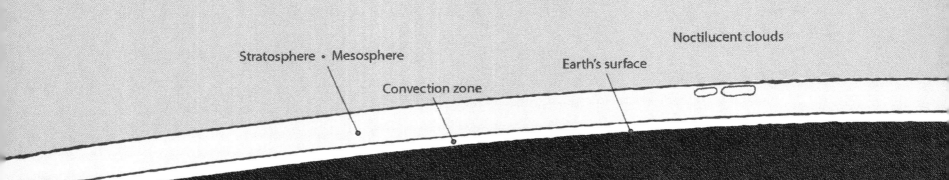

Scenery is a vast expanse.
Though it may appear vague and elusive,
scenery has a boundary.
Scenery extends between
curved ground and curved sky,
with these joining in the far distance.

This forms the horizon, and the boundary.
Scenery is a limited space
with both size and shape.
A huge, flat space.
Scenery is the largest space
able to be experienced on earth.

University Multipurpose Plaza

Think of a structure of similar
proportions to a scenery
looking towards the horizon.
An enormous roof
for a multipurpose plaza at a university.
A roof with an 80-meter span,
supported by the surrounding walls.

Not a single pillar.
One giant sheet of steel plate,
12 millimeters thick.
The average ceiling height
is about 2.3 meters.
A huge, flat space.

Apertures in the steel roof,
no glass in the openings,
let in the light
creating a huge, semi-outdoor space.

An enormous roof as sky.
Floor as land.

In the distance, they form a horizon.

University Multipurpose Plaza 271

Scenery that extends to the horizon,
as one gigantic space.

Though it appears uniformly cloudy,
in some places it is raining,
in others there are glimmers of light.

University Mult purpose Plaza

Different places appear
and disappear
according to the time of day
and weather.

University Multipurpose Plaza

A sunny day.
The openings in the steel roof
let in generous amounts of light.
Light from the high ceiling
fills the space evenly,
yet this is a very flat space.

The light does not circulate,
so it is only bright
around the openings.
Though one large space,
there are patches of
light and dark depending on location,
creating myriad kinds of spaces.

University Mutipurpose Plaza

On rainy days,
rain enters through the many openings.
Columns of rain appear indoors,
forming the scenery.
Views with falling rain,
and those without, mingle.

In one opening,
water gathers to form a waterfall.
Weather is produced,
outside is created
inside a piece of architecture.

Students head for this plaza
as if going on holiday.

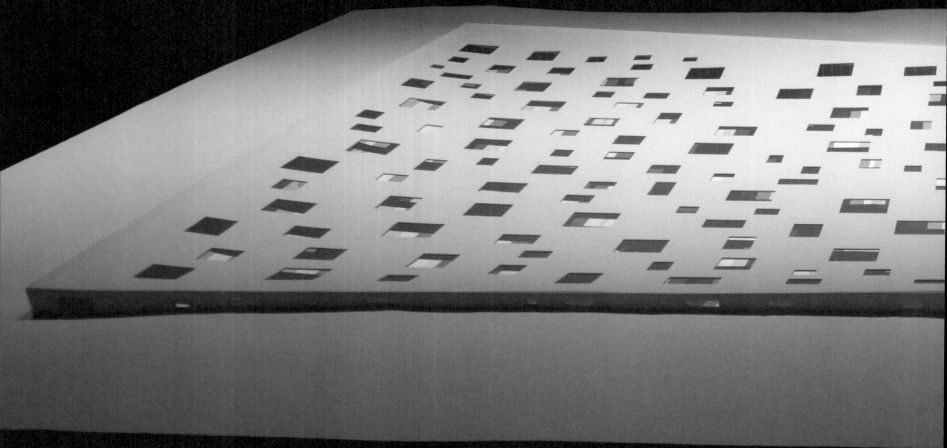

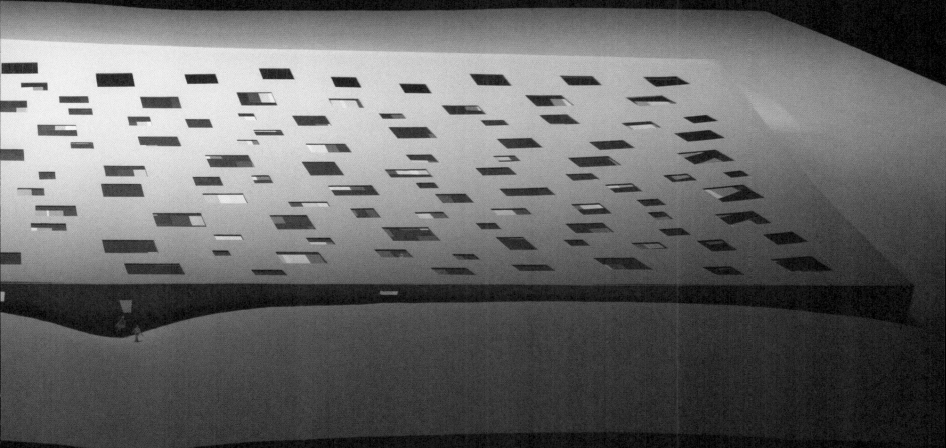

University Multipurpose Plaza

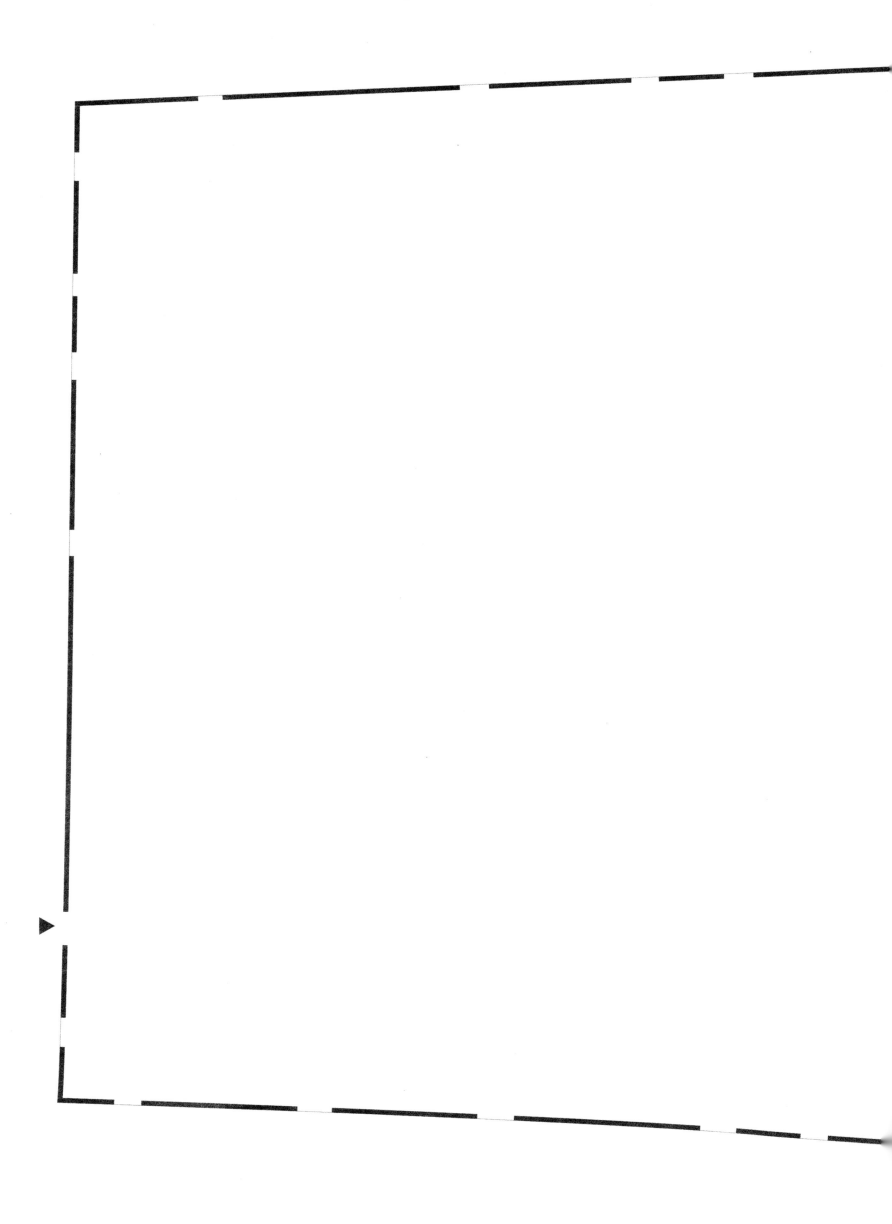

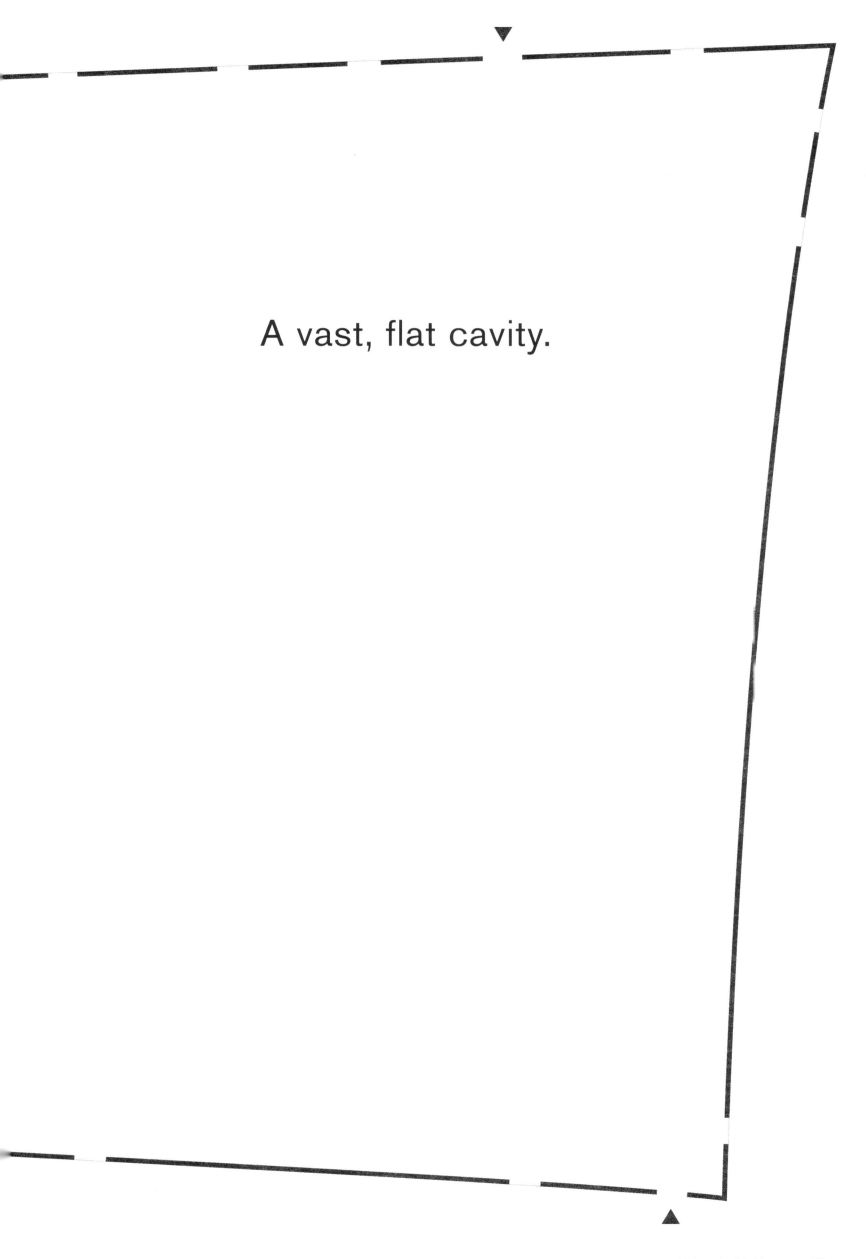

A vast, flat cavity.

University Multipurpose Plaza

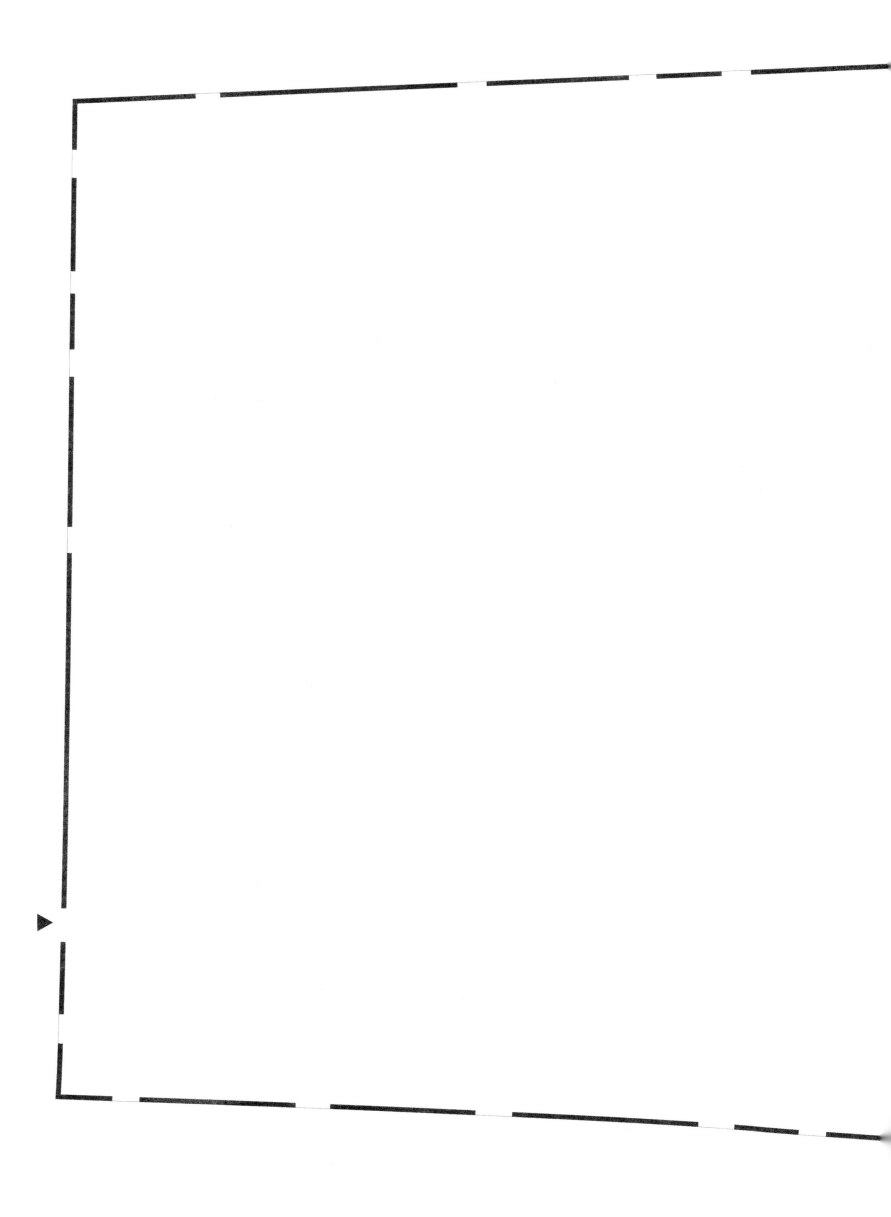

A ground plan
with nothing on it.

It may have nothing,
but it does have
size and shape.
Think of the
loosely defined space
of scenery.

University Multipurpose Plaza

The scenery of
the large garden on the south side.
The scenery of
a spacious tatami room.
The horizontal scenery of paddy fields
stretching into the distance.

Scenery strongly
imprinted on my memory,
where I sensed this place as
this place.
A house for my parents
and grandmother.

The site of
my grandmother's house,
in a corner of
what was once a farming village.
It was already very old,
and needed to be rebuilt.

My first home.

Taking the scenery sensed here
and making it the structure,
design a new house in which
it forms the backdrop.
Joining the scenery
to form a house.
Creating a continuous
backdrop to living.

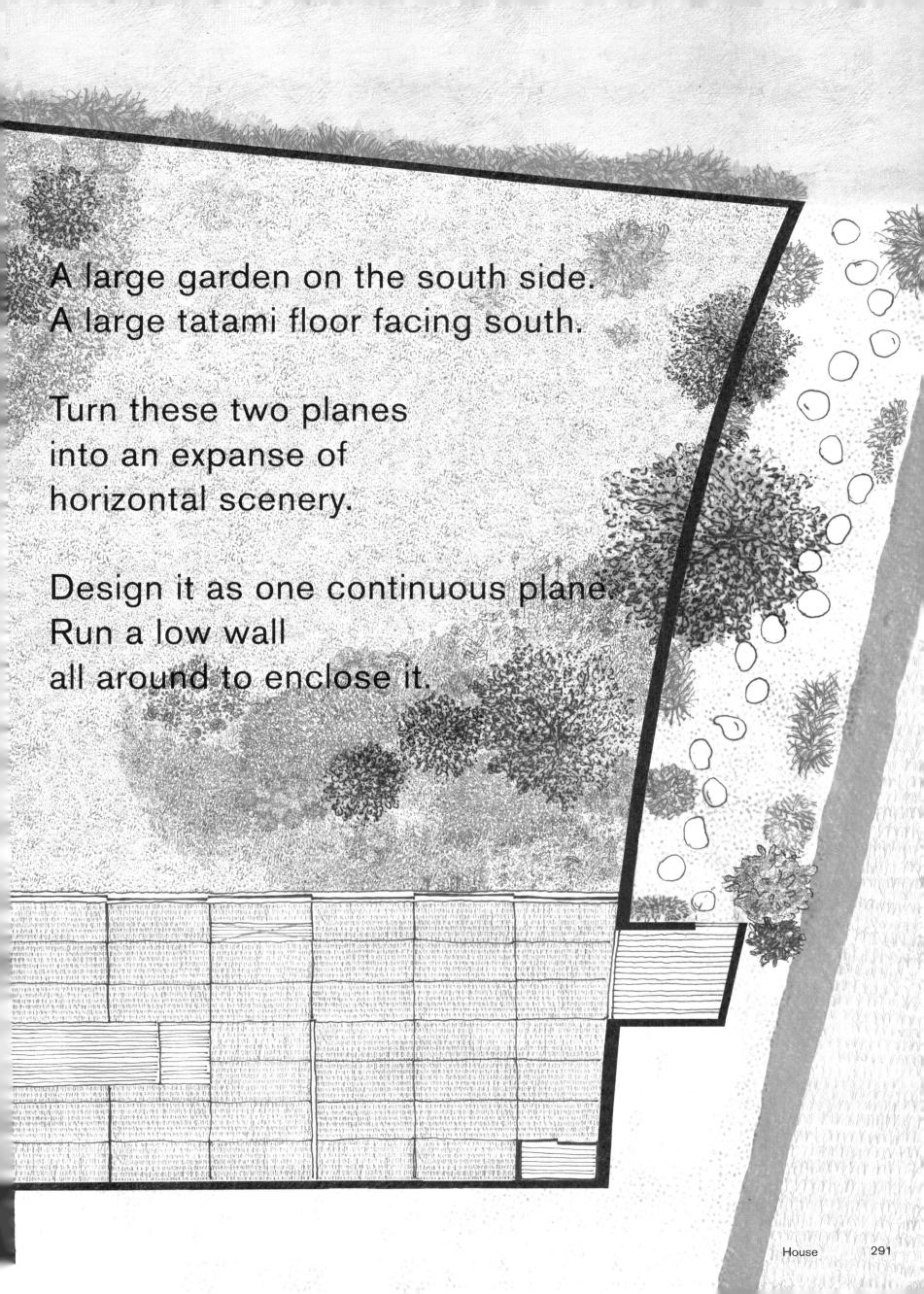

A large garden on the south side.
A large tatami floor facing south.

Turn these two planes
into an expanse of
horizontal scenery.

Design it as one continuous plane.
Run a low wall
all around to enclose it.

The wall higher at one end,
becoming lower towards the other end.
The garden is a slope with a slight curve.
Start at the same height as the tatami,
and at the edge, reach the height of the wall.
The wall vanishes into the ground.

The roof over the tatami
is a shed roof curving slightly
from the top of the wall,
becoming lower towards the garden.

In the garden, transplant trees
that have been present on the site
for a long time.

Plant flowers on the curved roof.
Eaves are below the line of sight.

Roof and ground form a single,
continuous garden,
embracing this place.

Thus making a garden
as extensive as before,
enclosed in hedge
and windbreak trees.

A very low, long window faces south.
A very horizontal window.
1.3 meters tall, 25 meters long.

The village scenery
has lost its integrity, with new houses
being built on either side.

A fence along the side path,
low-hanging eaves:
these will obscure the neighboring houses
different from earlier days.
The window will be filled solely
with a view of the south garden.

By the window.
Looking out over the fields.
Beyond the garden,
one can see the adjacent trees,
and, in the distance,
a mountain range.

Walking, stopping,
sitting on the floor,
sitting on a chair,
lying down, crouching,
standing up,
going out into the garden,
leaving the garden:
a landscape
that changes states subtly,
as if closely tracing
my parents' movements.

A landscape to connect
the scenery of memory,
and this place now.

Tatami as landscape,
long window as landscape,
low-hanging roof as landscape,
low wall as landscape,
south garden as landscape:
connecting to each other,
disconnecting,
altering each time,
with each experience.

These landscapes
are all designed
to be at a scale
within reach,
extensions of the
inhabitant's body.

Walking down the side path.
New wall joined seamlessly
with the same presence
as the existing hedge.
About head height.
A wall stretching low and far.
Scenery segueing horizontally.
With paddy fields extending beyond.

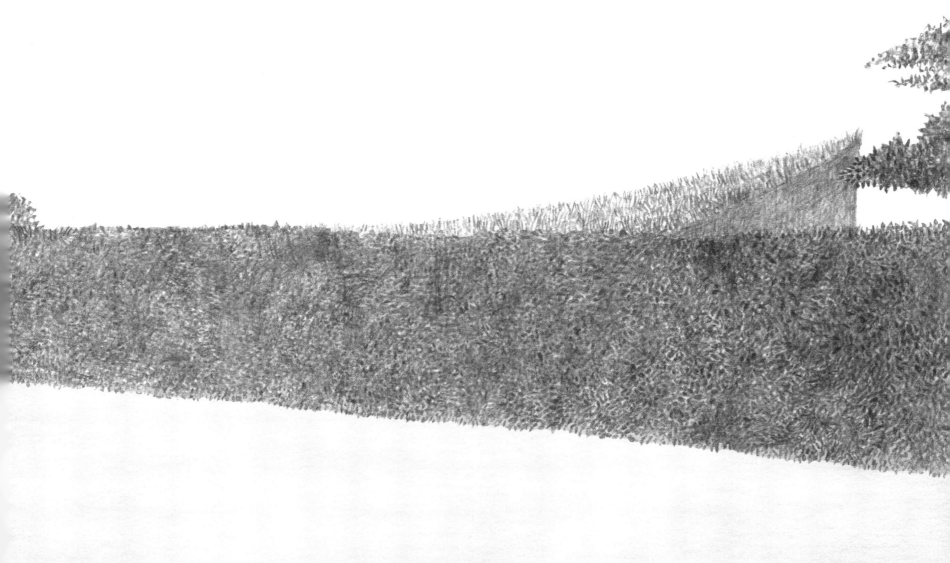

Freeing architecture
means listening carefully to,
observing,
what is already in this world,
and becoming knowledgable
about many things.

Engaging with what is
in front of us.

The flexibility to discard
fixed ideas,
and accept what is there,
for what it is.

Becoming liberated from
our personal values.

Scenery.

A multitude of scenery
joins together,
forming the world;
the huge space
we call the world.

If architects,
and non-architects,
from all over,
people all around the world,
could think about architecture
more freely.

If such scenery joined
together to form a single space,
the world would be all the richer for it.

The different values in the world
and types of architecture in the world
would come closer together.

Architecture would become
more intimate than it is now.

Architecture for an age of free access to information.

Architecture for an age of free connections.

Architecture for an age of freedom in values.

The handful of projects shown here
are small examples of all this.

Freeing architecture.

Project Information

House with Plants
Program: Residence
Location: East Japan
Total floor area: 99.8m²
Number of floors: 1 story + mezzanine
Structure: Steel
Project architects: Junya Ishigami,
Akira Uchimura, Sachie Morita
Structural engineers:
Jun Sato Structural Engineers
Horticulture: Equipe Espace
Textile coordination: Yoko Ando Design
Period: 2010–2012
≫ p. 014

**Botanical Garden Art Biotop /
Water Garden**
Program: Garden
Location: Tochigi, Japan
Total site area: 16,670m²
Project architects: Junya Ishigami,
Eiko Tomura, Taeko Abe, Lucie Loosen,
Gaku Inoue, Akira Uchimura
Contractor: Shizuoka Green Service Co.
Period: 2013–2018
≫ p. 028

Kids Park
Program: Interior park
Location: East Japan
Total floor area: 2,264m²
Project architects: Junya Ishigami,
Kei Sato, Taeko Abe
Structural engineers:
Jun Sato Structural Engineers
Period: 2013–
≫ p. 126

Cloud Garden
Program: Interior park, nursery room,
parenting support center
Location: Kanagawa, Japan
Total floor area: 2,264m²
Project architects: Junya Ishigami,
Kei Sato, Taeko Abe, Shuma Tei,
Eiko Tomura, Kazuyuki Takeda
Structural engineers:
Jun Sato Structural Engineers
Contractor: Atelier Umi +
Maeda Sanno Dokyo JV
Period: 2013–2014
≫ p. 138

House & Restaurant
Program: Residence, restaurant
Location: Yamaguchi, Japan
Total floor area: 194.0m²
Number of floors: 1 story
Structure: Concrete
Project architects: Junya Ishigami,
Kei Sato, Taeko Abe, Atsushi Sato
Structural engineers:
Jun Sato Structural Engineers
Contractor: Akita Co., Inc.
Period: 2013–
≫ p. 210

Chapel of Valley
Program: Chapel
Location: Shandong, China
Total floor area: 132m²
Number of floors: 1 story
Structure: Concrete
Project architects: Junya Ishigami,
Zenan Li, Cing Lu, Taeko Abe,
Akira Uchimura, Kei Sato
Partner architects: CCDI Group
Structural engineers:
Jun Sato Structural Engineers, CCDI Group
Contractor: Beijing YiHuiDa Fair-faced
Concrete Company
Period: 2016–
≫ p. 240

Park Groot Vijversburg Visitor Center
Program: Visitor center
Location: Tytsjerk, The Netherlands
Total floor area: 245m² (new construction), 350m² (renovation)
Number of floors: 1 story (new construction), 3 stories (renovation)
Structure: Glass, steel
Project architects: Junya Ishigami, Wataru Shinji, Akira Uchimura, Terutaka Ide, Shuma Tei, Taeko Abe
Partner architects:
Studio Maks / Marieke Kums
Structural engineers:
Jun Sato Structural Engineers, ABT
Contractor: Jurriens Noord & Friso Bouwgroep
Period: 2012–2017
≫ p. 046

Home for the Elderly
Program: Group home
Location: Tohoku, Japan
Total floor area: 560m²
Number of floors: 1 story
Structure: Wood
Project architects: Junya Ishigami, Yuichi Uehara, Takashi Matsuda, Akihiro Yamaya
Structural engineers:
Jun Sato Structural Engineers
Facility design: ES ASSOCIATES
Period: 2012–
≫ p. 064

Polytechnic Museum
Program: Museum
Location: Moscow, Russia
Total floor area: 39,870m²
Number of floors: 6 stories
Structure: Brick, steel, concrete
Project architects: Junya Ishigami, Alexandra Kovaleva, Wataru Shinji, Soichi Inami, Kei Sato, Kevin Walsh, Taeko Abe, Yuki Horikoshi
Period: 2012–
≫ p. 090

8 Villas in Dali
Program: Villas
Location: Dali, China
Total floor area: 5,000m²
Number of floors: 1 story
Structure: Stone, concrete
Project architects: Junya Ishigami, Zenan Li, Taeko Abe, Jaehyub Ko, Tong Zhang
Structural engineers:
Jun Sato Structural Engineers
Period: 2016–
≫ p. 110

Forest Kindergarten
Program: Kindergarten
Location: Shandong, China
Total floor area: 5,400m²
Number of floors: 1 story
Structure: Steel, concrete
Project architects: Junya Ishigami, Alexandra Kovaleva, Zenan Li, Wataru Shinji, Taeko Abe, Akira Uchimura, Gagas Firas Silmi
Structural engineers:
Jun Sato Structural Engineers, CCDI Group
Period: 2015–
≫ p. 144

Cloud Arch
Program: Urban monument
Location: Sydney, Australia
Structure: Steel
Project architects: Junya Ishigami, Wataru Shinji, Taeko Abe, Masayuki Asami
Partner architects: Partridge Event
Structural engineers: Partridge Event, Jun Sato Structural Engineers
Period: 2015–
≫ p. 162

KAIT Workshop
Program: Educational facility, university atelier
Location: Kanagawa, Japan
Total floor area: 1,989.15m²
Number of floors: 1 story
Structure: Steel
Project architects: Junya Ishigami, Motosuke Mandai, Sachie Morita, Harushi Chousa
Structural engineers:
Konishi Structural Engineers
Facility design: Environmental Engineers
Contractor: Kajima Corporation
Period: 2004–2008
≫ p. 180

House of Peace
Program: Space for personal reflection and meditation
Location: Copenhagen, Denmark
Total floor area: 3,000m²
Number of floors: 1 story
Structure: Concrete
Project architects: Junya Ishigami, Wataru Shinji, Tei Sauma, Taeko Abe, Takashi Matsuda, Eico Tomura
Partner architects: Srendborg Architects
Structural engineers:
Jun Sato Structural Engineers
Environmental engineers:
Transsolar | KlimaEngineering
Period: 2014–
≫ p. 196

Cultural Center
Program: Cultural center
Location: Shandong, China
Total floor area: 3000m²
Number of floors: 1 story
Structure: Steel, concrete
Project architects: Junya Ishigami, Zenan Li, Zhi Rui Lim, Rui Xu, Tong Zhang, Sellua Di Ceglie
Partner architects: CCDI Group
Structural engineers:
Jun Sato Structural Engineers, CCDI Group
Period: 2016–
≫ p. 254

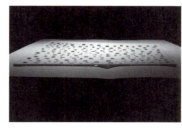

University Multipurpose Plaza
Program: Multipurpose plaza
Location: Kanagawa, Japan
Total floor area: 4,109m²
Number of floors: 1 story
Structure: Steel
Project architects: Junya Ishigami, Kei Sato, Taeko Abe, Shuma Tei, Motosuke Mandai, Sachie Morita, Toru Yamada
Structural engineers:
Jun Sato Structural Engineers
Contractor: Kajima Corporation
Period: 2008–
≫ p. 266

House
Program: Residence
Location: East Japan
Total floor area: 128.5m²
Number of floors: 1 story
Structure: Concrete, steel
Project architects: Junya Ishigami, Akira Uchimura, Taeko Abe, Masayuki Asami
Structural engineers:
Jun Sato Structural Engineers
Period: 2013–
≫ p. 288

Image Credits

4–13
© JUNYA.ISHIGAMI+ASSOCIATES

House with Plants
14–27
© JUNYA.ISHIGAMI+ASSOCIATES

**Botanical Farm Garden
Art Biotop / Water Garden**
28–45
© JUNYA.ISHIGAMI+ASSOCIATES

**Park Groot Vijversburg
Visitor Center**
52–53
Photograph by Laurian Ghinitoiu
54–57, 313
Photographs by Giovanni Emilio
Galanello
46–51, 58–63
© JUNYA.ISHIGAMI+ASSOCIATES

Home for the Elderly
64–65
Mirei Shigemori, *Jissokuzu:
nihon no meien*
(Tokyo, Seibundoshinkosha) 1971.
72
Photograph by Yasuhiro Takagi
66–71, 73–89
© JUNYA.ISHIGAMI+ASSOCIATES

Polytechnic Museum
90–91
'The discovery of the temple of Isis at
Pompeii, buried under pumice
and other volcanic matter. Coloured
etching by Pietro Fabris, 1776.'
by Pietro Fabris. Wellcome
Collection. CC BY
92–93
Photograph by Loskutov, Soyuzphoto,
1935
94–109
© JUNYA.ISHIGAMI+ASSOCIATES

8 Villas in Dali
110–25
© JUNYA.ISHIGAMI+ASSOCIATES

Kids Park
126–37
© JUNYA.ISHIGAMI+ASSOCIATES

Cloud Garden
138–43
© JUNYA.ISHIGAMI+ASSOCIATES

Forest Kindergarten
144–61
© JUNYA.ISHIGAMI+ASSOCIATES

Cloud Arch
162–79
© JUNYA.ISHIGAMI+ASSOCIATES

**Kanagawa Institute of
Technology Workshop**
180–81
Ball, R. S., An *Atlas of Astronomy:
A Series of seventy-two plates*
(London, George Philip) 1892.
188–89
Makoto Numata, *Seitaigaku no
tachiba* (Tokyo, Kokinshoin) 1958.
182–87, 192–95
© JUNYA.ISHIGAMI+ASSOCIATES

House of Peace
196–97
Clouds above a calm sea.
Painting by Ivan Aivazovsky, 1889.
198–209
© JUNYA.ISHIGAMI+ASSOCIATES

House & Restaurant
232–37
Photographs by Satoru Emoto
210–31, 238–39
© JUNYA.ISHIGAMI+ASSOCIATES

Chapel of Valley
240–41
Colange, Leo de, *The Heart
of Europe: From the Rhine to
the Danube* (Boston,
Estes and Lauriat) 1882.
242–52
© JUNYA.ISHIGAMI+ASSOCIATES

Cultural Center
254–65
© JUNYA.ISHIGAMI+ASSOCIATES

University Multipurpose Plaza
282–83
Hamblyn, Richard,
*Extraordinary Clouds:
Skies of the unexpected from
the beautiful to the bizarre*
(Cincinnati, David & Charles Limited)
2009.
266–71, 274–81, 284–87
© JUNYA.ISHIGAMI+ASSOCIATES

House
288–303
© JUNYA.ISHIGAMI+ASSOCIATES

In reproducing the images contained in this publication, LIXIL Publishing obtained
the permission of the rights holders whenever possible. Should LIXIL Publishing
have been unable to locate the rights holder, notwithstanding good-faith efforts, it
requests that any contact information concerning such rights holders be forwarded
so that they may be contacted for future editions.

Junya Ishigami

1974	Born in Kanagawa, Japan
2000	M.F.A. in Architecture,
	Tokyo National University of Fine Arts and Music
2000-04	Joined Kazuyo Sejima & Associates
2004	Established JUNYA.ISHIGAMI+ASSOCIATES
2014	Visiting Professor at Harvard University, USA
2015	Visiting Professor at Princeton University, USA
2016	Visiting Professor at Academy of Architecture of Mendrisio,
	Switzerland
2017	Visiting Professor at The Oslo School
	of Architecture and Design, Norway
2017	Visiting Professor at Columbia University, USA

Awards

2005	SD Prize, SD Review 2005
2008	Iakov Chernikhov Prize 2008
2008	Kanagawa Cultural Award
2009	contractworld.award 2009
2009	Bauwelt Prize 2009
2009	Architectural Institute of Japan Prize 2009
2009	BCS Prize
2010	Golden Lion award in part of the 12th International
	Architecture Exhibition, La Biennale di Venezia
2010	Mainichi Design Awards 2010
2016	BSI Swiss Architectural Award

Published works

Tables as small architecture, Gallery Koyanagi, 2006
plants & architecture,
JUNYA.ISHIGAMI+ASSOCIATES, 2008
small images, LIXIL Publishing, 2008
balloon & garden, Daiwa Press, 2010
Another scale of architecture, Seigensha, 2010
How small? How vast? How architecture grows,
Shiseido Gallery, 2011; Hatje Cantz Verlag, 2013

Acknowledgments

The Fondation Cartier pour l'art contemporain is profoundly grateful to Junya Ishigami for entrusting its team with his first major solo show as well as for his determination and vision in accomplishing this ambitious project. Throughout this endeavor, his intellectual rigor, artistic inventiveness, and breadth of view have greatly inspired us.

Our deepest gratitude also goes to the team of JUNYA.ISHIGAMI +ASSOCIATES, and in particular to Wataru Shinji and Lily Zhang, for their unfailing commitment to this project. Their dedication was critical to the success of this undertaking.

We would particularly like to thank Hitomi Kitayama, Yokozawa Farm Inc.; Kenichiro Nakabe, Ikutoku Gakuen / Kanagawa Institute of Technology; Kasper Winding, HOPE Foundation; and Qunde Xu, Shandong Rizhao Bailuan Town, for providing support for the production and exhibition of the models.

We extend our thanks to Atsuko Koyanagi, Director of the Gallery Koyanagi, and to Naoko Kawamura, with whom we have shared our passion for Junya Ishigami's work over many years.

We wish to express our appreciation to everyone whose technical advice and dedication helped us in the preparation of the exhibition:

Adhequat
L'Aquarium de Paris - Cinéaqua
Atelier Boutin
Atelier Devineau
Bâches de France
Grappa Studio
Groupe Coutant
Paris Bonzaï
Paris vert Ouest

Finally, we would like to express our profound gratitude to everyone who, in various ways, contributed to the exhibition and the catalog.

JUNYA.ISHIGAMI+ASSOCIATES would like to express our sincere gratitude to Hervé Chandès and Isabelle Gaudefroy for sharing the opportunity and the conviction to achieve this exhibition together. We also extend our deepest appreciation to the entire team of the Fondation Cartier pour l'art contemporain, without whom this project would not be possible, and to all those who contributed to the realization of this exhibition and the catalog.

Freeing Architecture (Japanese: *Jiyu na kenchiku*) was the title of the author's essay published in the "Architectural Theory" column of the January 2011 edition of the magazine *Shin kenchiku* (Shinkenchikusha), which formed the basis of the concept for this exhibition. Once again, we would like to thank the many people who assisted with this endeavor.

By & Havn
City of Atsugi
City of Sydney
Dali Yangbi Shimenguan Tourism
    Development
Dreyers Fond
Fondation Cartier pour l'art
    contemporain
HOPE Foundation
Ikutoku Gakuen / Kanagawa
    Institute of Technology
LIXIL, LIXIL Publishing
nikissimo Inc.
Park Vijversburg
Politiken Fonden
Polytechnic Museum
    Development Foundation
restaurant Noël
Shandong Rizhao Bailuan Town
Takara Leben Co., Ltd.
Yokozawa Farm Inc.

Toshiharu Abe
Mitsuru Chiba
Satoru Emoto
Giovanni Emilio Galanello
Laurian Ghinitoiu
Seiwa Hada
Motonori Hirata
Yasushi Ichikawa
Gaku Inoue
Daisuke Kano
Ryo Kitagawa
Hitomi Kitayama
Miyu Kitayama
Masataka Kiyono
Kenji Kobayashi
Masao Kodama
Hitoshi Koyama
Masahiko Kubota
Chinatsu Kuma
Katsuhiro Kumaki
Pamela Miki
Takashi Miyazaki
Kenichiro Nakabe
Shuichi Nakazato
Atsuko Nishimaki
Fumikazu Ohara
Kayoko Ota
Mitsuhiro Saka
Jun Sato
Makoto Sato
Masahiro Sato
Natsumi Sato
Yutaka Shikata
Yasuhiro Takagi
Toshihiko Takeda
Hiroyuki Uehara
Kenji Uehara
Koji Uehara
Kasper Winding
Qunde Xu

Marco Antrodicchia
Daehwa Baek
Laurane Barry
Inga Baufale
Titien Brendlé
Alfonso Cano Abarca
Marta Cavallé
Clarisse Cheung
Valentina Chiesa
Jordi Costa Ritas
Tim Cousin
Maya Dann
Héloïse Darves-Bornoz
Patrick de Almeida Lothoz
Morgan Delvauz
Walter Fu
Maxence Granceot
Xiangyu Guo
Atsushi Hiruma
Tiffany Hon
Omar Imadioun
Malene Prytz Larsen
Sabrina Leung
Eytan Levi
Jacques Ligot
Haidee Lim
Léa Mancini
Ran Mei
Dilara Murzagalyeva
Naoki Ono
Gabriele Pagan
Yue Pan
Alexandre Paul
Noël Picaper
Arthur Randé
Mathilde Redoué
Ludovico Scarlini
Angad Sharma
Harsh Pratap Singh
Regina Stolz
Connie Lynn Targ
Stien Verheye
Martha Virgaux
Wen Wang
Kenneth Wu

JUNYA.ISHIGAMI+ASSOCIATES
Exhibition and Catalog Team

Junya Ishigami
Wataru Shinji
Lily Zhang

Masayuki Asami
Sellua Di Ceglie
Munehiro Fukushima
Alexandra Kovaleva
Atsushi Sato
Kei Sato
Gagas Firas Silmi
Yuki Sudo
Cong Xia
Tong Zhang

This catalog was published
in conjunction with the exhibition
Junya Ishigami, Freeing Architecture,
presented at the Fondation Cartier
pour l'art contemporain in Paris
from March 30 to June 10, 2018.

EXHIBITION

Fondation Cartier pour l'art contemporain

General Director: Hervé Chandès
Curator: Isabelle Gaudefroy assisted by Laure Chauvelot
Production: Camille Chenet and Victoire Guéna
assisted by Claire Pierson
Technical Coordinator: Vincent Lecerf assisted by Kei Furukata
Registrar: Corinne Bocquet assisted by Alanna Minta Jordan,
Paola Sisterna, and Akara Yagi
Lighting: Gérald Karlikow
Signage: Jessica Chèze and Justine Gautier
Graphic Design (signage): Agnès Dahan and Raphaëlle Piquet,
Agnès Dahan Studio, Paris

CATALOG

Published on March 30, 2018

LIXIL Publishing, Tokyo

Corporate Director: Yoko Satake
Director: Chinatsu Kuma

Editor: Lily Zhang
Designer: SOUP DESIGN
Translation from Japanese: Pamela Miki

Fondation Cartier pour l'art contemporain, Paris

Editorial Manager: Adeline Pelletier
Editorial Project Coordinator: Cécile Provost
Editorial Assistant: Iris Aleluia
Proofreading: Bronwyn Mahoney

FONDATION CARTIER POUR L'ART CONTEMPORAIN

President: Alain Dominique Perrin

General Director: Hervé Chandès
External Relations Manager: Pauline Duclos
Assistant to the General Director: Bérengère Landron

Director of Programing and Artistic Projects: Isabelle Gaudefroy
Assistant to the Director: Leïla Bouchra

Curators: Thomas Delamarre, Marie Perennes, and Leanne Sacramone
Curatorial Assistants: Laure Chauvelot and Juan Ignacio Luque Soto
Interns: Sarah Caillet and Anne-Fleur Merlaud

Exhibition Production Manager: Camille Chenet and Victoire Guéna
Production Assistant: Claire Pierson
Technical Coordinator: Vincent Lecerf

Nomadic Nights Manager: Mélanie Alves de Sousa
Nomadic Nights Production Coordinator: Agathe Robert
Nomadic Nights Production Assistant: Lucie Jeannenot
Intern: Elsa Brunet-Masson

Publications Manager: Adeline Pelletier
Editors: Nolwen Lauzanne and Pierre-Édouard Couton
Editorial Project Coordinator: Cécile Provost
Editorial Assistants: Iris Aleluia and Aubane Favier

Director of Collections: Grazia Quaroni
Curator of the Collections: Lauriane Gricourt
Collections Assistant: Lilit Sokhakyan and Qian Kun

Communications and Development Director: Naïa Sore
Communications and Development Deputy Director: Laurène Blottière
Internal Communications and External Relations Coordinator:
Johanne Legris
Department Assistant: Philippine Aubert

Editorial Communications Manager: Jessica Chèze
Editorial Project Coordinator: Justine Gautier
Assistant: Claire Corneloup

Digital Project Coordinator: Nicolas Rapp
Digital Content and Audiovisual Production Coordinator: Lucie Lerat
Intern: Valentin Guérin

Press Manager: Matthieu Simonnet
Press Officers: Maïté Perrocheau and Léa Soghomonian

Bookshop and Visitor Services Manager: Vania Merhar
Department Assistant: Marcel Badan
Visitor Services Assistant: Aline Feldbrugge

Administrative and Financial Director: Caroline Valentin
Administrative and Financial Deputy Director: Zoé Clémot
Financial Manager of Operations: Jade Bouchemit
Accounting and Payroll Manager: Fabienne Pommier
Administrative Assistant: Aurore Guilbaud

Registrar Manager: Corinne Bocquet
Registrar: Alanna Minta Jordan
Registrar Assistant: Paola Sisterna and Akara Yagi
Technical Registrar: Gilles Gioan
Gardener: Metin Sevrin

The exhibition *Junya Ishigami, Freeing Architecture* was organized with
support from the Fondation Cartier pour l'art contemporain,
under the aegis of the Fondation de France, and with he sponsorship
of Cartier.

© Junya Ishigami for the texts and works
© 2018, LIXIL Publishing, Tokyo /
Fondation Cartier pour l'art contemporain, Paris

All rights reserved. No part of this publication may be reproduced or
transmitted in any form or by any means. electronic or mechanical,
including photocopy, recording or any other storage and retrieval
system, without prior permission in writing from the publishers.

Printed and bound in Japan in 2018 by SANEI PRINTERY.

LIXIL Publishing, LIXIL Corporation
3-6-18 Kyobashi, Chuo-ku, Tokyo
104-0031, JAPAN
www1.lixil.co.jp/publish
ISBN: 978-4-86480-037-2
ISBN: 978-4-86480-036-5

Fondation Cartier pour l'art contemporain
261, boulevard Raspail, 75014 Paris
fondation.cartier.com
ISBN: 978-2-86925-133-5
Legal deposit: Bibliothègue Nationale de France, March 2018

本書は、パリのカルティエ現代美術館で開催された
個展「JUNYA ISHIGAMI, Freeing Architecture」
(2018年3月30日～6月10日)に合わせて、カルティ
エ現代美術館との共同出版により刊行された。

JUNYA ISHIGAMI: FREEING ARCHITECTURE

2018年3月28日 第1刷発行

著者　　　石上純也

発行者　　佐竹葉子
発行所　　LIXIL出版
　　　　　104-0031 東京都中央区京橋3-6-18
　　　　　Tel: 03-5250-6571 Fax: 03-5250-6549
　　　　　www1.lixil.co.jp/publish

編集協力　リリー・ゼン
デザイン　尾原史和
　　　　　加納大輔
　　　　　(SOUP DESIGN)

印刷製本　三永印刷

乱丁・落丁本は小社までお送りください。
送料小社負担にてお取替えいたします。

ISBN 978-4-86480-037-2　C0052
© 2018, Junya Ishigami　Printed in Japan
© 2018, LIXIL Publishing, Tokyo /
Fondation Cartier pour l'art contemporain, Paris

Contemporary Music of Japan

SERAPHIM
for Violin and Orchestra

Harue KUNIEDA

現代日本の音楽

セラフィム
ヴァイオリンとオーケストラのための

国枝春恵

音楽之友社

ONGAKU NO TOMO EDITION

〔Instrumentation〕

2 Flutes (2nd doubling on Piccolo)

2 Oboes

2 Clarinets in B♭

2 Bassoons (2nd doubling on Double-Bassoon)

4 French horns in F

2 Trumpets in C

2 Trombones (Tenor)

1 Trombone (Bass)

1 Harp

1 Piano

Timpani

3 Percussion players

1st | 2 Suspended Cymbals (l. m.), 1 Chinese Cymbal, 2 Tam-tams (l. m.), Thai-Gongs

2nd | 3 Mokushōs (h. m. l.), 3 Wood Blocks (h. m. l.), 1 Pair of Bongos, Conga, 3 Tom-toms, Bass Drum, 1 Suspended Cymbal (m)

3rd | Tubular Bells, Vibraphone, Glockenspiel

Solo Violin

12 Violins I

12 Violins II

10 Violas

6 Violoncellos

6 Double basses

〔Abbreviations and Symbols〕

N. V. = non vibrato

V. = vibrato

S. P. = sul ponticello

S. T. = sul tasto

P. O. = posizione ordinario

T. = près de la table

= pizzicato à la Bartók

= scratch with the sticks

⊕ = mute the strings with the fingers

= strike the body of the instrument

◆ = blow into the tube

= sustain

= tie

= accelerando

= ritardando

= fade out

= sneak in

= the highest possible speed

↑ = the highest possible note

↓ = the lowest possible note

= glissando

= repeat the indicated notes at will

<Sticks>

s = soft   ord = ordinary   h = hard   m = metal   w = wooden   B = wire brush   b = D. B.'s bow

〔Duration: ca.15 minutes〕

初演：2000年3月2日　東京文化会館大ホール

ヴァイオリン：山崎貴子

指揮：渡邊一正　管弦楽：東京フィルハーモニー交響楽団

First performance on : March 2, 2000 at Tokyo Bunka Kaikan Main Hall.

Violin: Takako Yamasaki

Conductor: Kazumasa Watanabe, Tokyo Philharmonic Orchestra

Seraphim for Violin and Orchestra

国枝春恵
Harue KUNIEDA

©1999 by Harue Kunieda.
©2017 assigned to ONGAKU NO TOMO SHA CORP., Tokyo, Japan.

15

16

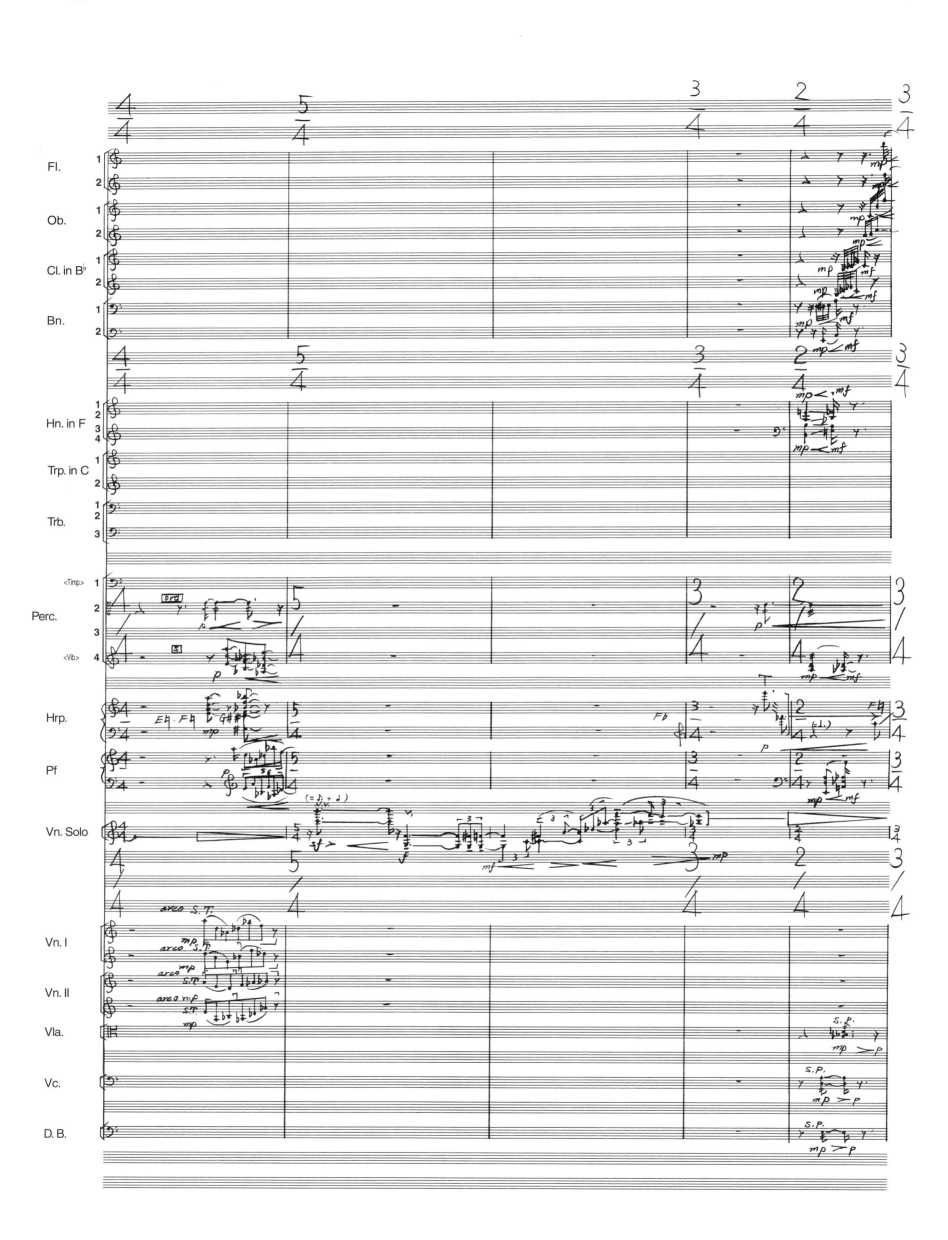

18

[Double Basson]
rapidly
[Thai - Gongs]
ord
cluster
8bass
8va
n.v.
s.p.
P.O.

20

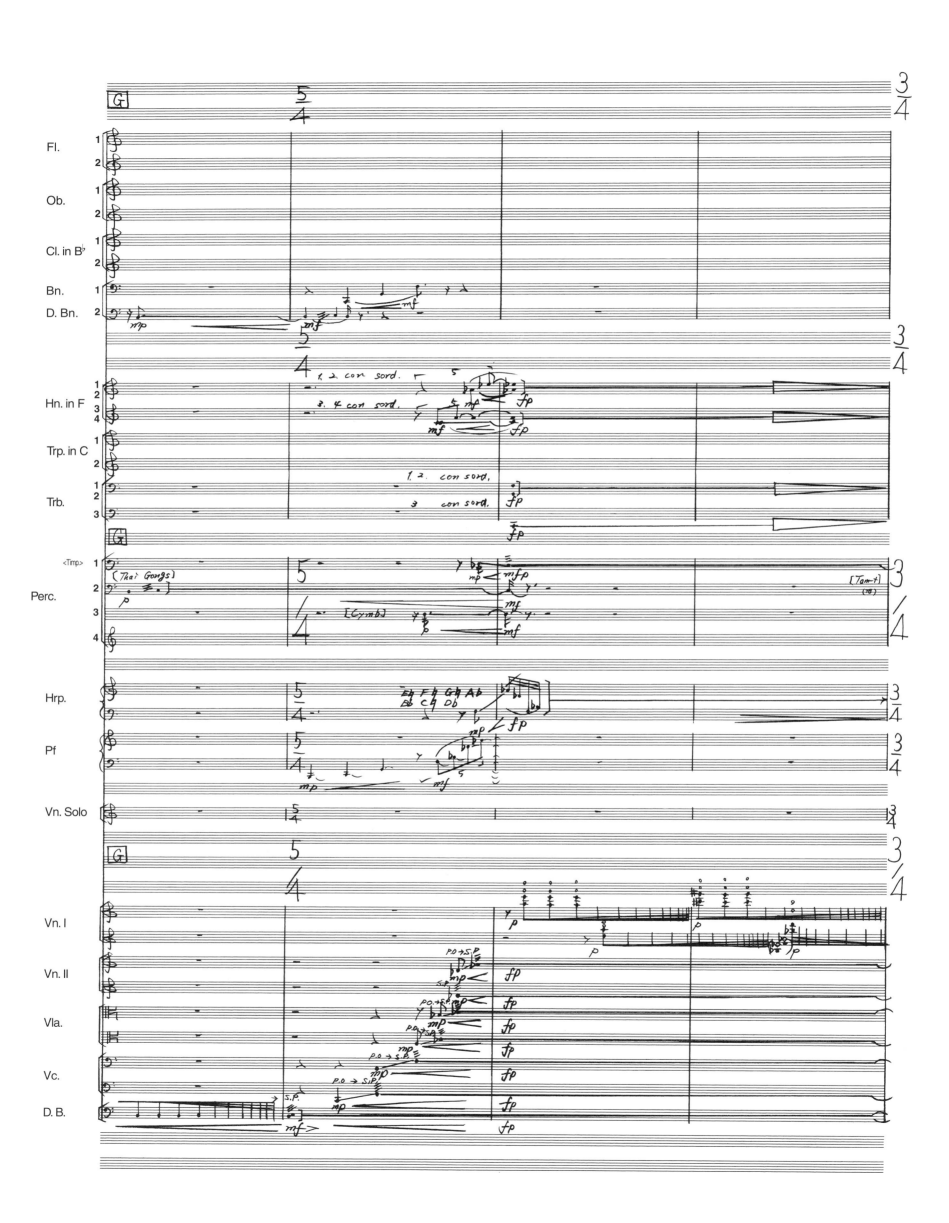

26

45

ヴァイオリンとオーケストラのための セラフィム
国枝 春恵

ヴァイオリンとオーケストラの作品を書くという構想は、既に何年も前から私の中で脈打っていた。1997年春には殆ど完成していたが、初演に際し、1999年夏に少々改訂し、カデンツァを含む現在の形態に至った。

冒頭の動機、音構造等は、ヴァイオリン・ソロのための《エレヴァシオン》（1985）とソプラノとハープのための《セレナーデ》（1992）と関連していて、それらは延長、増幅、拡大しながらも新たな音像の場を展開する。ヴァイオリンの緊張感溢れるドラマティックな音型は執拗に繰り返され、上昇、高揚する。オーケストラは、ソリストを包囲する音響を形成したり、対峙する空間を提示したりする。ヴァイオリン冒頭のE♭音、オーケストラ・トゥッティのH音、ピアノ・ハープのB♭・F完全五度音等は、暗示的な警鐘として全体の核を成している。

以前、私の家には、弾き手を失って嘆いているヴァイオリンがあった。私が、新しい作品の構想に集中して行くと、そのヴァイオリンの開放弦の音が唸った瞬間があった。その不思議な偶然は、私の作品に続いている強迫観念のような音であり、その後の私の作品の中でずっと鳴り続けている。それは、人間の内的葛藤と苦渋の情念が込められたドラマのようでもあった。私は、セラフィムが出現して、その上に救済の光が到来することを想定したのである。

「セラフィム」（熾天使 Seraphim）は、旧約聖書に記されている神に仕える最高位の天使であり、6つの羽を持ち、複数で飛び交い、神の栄光を讃え、全知を体現し、預言者達に言葉を与えた。この作品の終焉で、ヴァイオリニストの頭上に舞い降りてくる天使達を知覚することができたら……と願う。

国枝春恵

東京生まれ。1981年東京藝術大学音楽学部作曲科卒業、'83年同大学院作曲専攻修了。作曲を池内友次郎、野田暉行各氏に師事。
作品は、ISCM-ACL香港大会、オーストラリア大会、イスラエル大会、アジア音楽祭仙台、タングルウッド現代音楽祭等で演奏されている。ソプラノとハープのための《セレナーデ》は、2000年ISCM「世界の音楽の日々」ルクセンブルク大会に入選。2003年文化庁特別派遣在外研修員。2005年N響ミュージック・トゥモロー委嘱作品《地上の平和》は、2009年ISCM「世界の音楽の日々」スウェーデン大会に入選し、再演されている。2010年アンサンブルMD 7委嘱作品《レシテーションⅢ》は、スロヴェニア、ウニクム音楽祭、イタリア、トリエステ・プリマ音楽祭で初演されている。
現在、熊本大学教育学部教授、日本現代音楽協会、21世紀音楽の会各会員
http://www.harue-kunieda.com

Seraphim for Violin and Orchestra
Harue KUNIEDA

I thought about writing a new piece for the violin and an orchestra for a long time.

I completed it in the spring of 1997, though it was partly revised in the summer of 1999, including the violin's cadenza.

The tone structure and motif of the beginning concern *Élévation pour Violon Solo* (1985) and *Serenade for Soprano and Harp* (1992). They lead to a new sound scape increasing, widening and repeating. The violin's dramatic motif and tension are repeated persistently and excitedly. The orchestra makes acoustic surrounding which the violinist collaborates with and plays opposite to. The focus of the whole piece is a cautionary bell sounding. It shows up in the piece as the E♭ tone in the beginning of the violin, the B tone in the orchestra's tutti, the complete 5th of the B♭ tone and the F tone in the piano and the harp.

There was a special violin in my house which seemed to be deploring the fact that nobody played it any longer. I was focusing on that violin as part of conceiving a new piece when an open string began to hum. I felt moved by that magical coincidence and was compelled to use that sound in my piece. It had a lasting influence on my subsequent work. It seemed to represent a kind of drama of inner conflict and touch on the painful pathos of human life. I imagined the appearance of Seraphim coming to relieve the problem with their light from above.

"Seraphim" are the greatest angels of The Old Testament, having six wings, flying together, praising the glory of God, seeing the Almighty, and giving god's words to the prophets.

At the end of this piece, we can feel that the angels have swept down quietly onto the violin's head.

Harue KUNIEDA

Born in Tokyo, she entered the Tokyo University of the Arts and majored in composition, graduating in 1983.
Her works have been performed at ISCM-ACL in Hong Kong, Australia and Israel, at the Asian Music Festival in Sendai, at Tanglewood Contemporary Music Festival and others. *Serenade for Soprano and Harp* was selected for ISCM World Music Days in Luxemburg in 2000. She was an artist of the Japanese Government Overseas Study Program in London in 2003. *Peace on Earth for Soprano, Harp and Orchestra* was commissioned and the first performed by the NHK Symphony Orchestra in Tokyo in 2005, was selected for ISCM World New Music Days in Sweden in 2009. *Recitation III for Seven Players* was commissioned and performed by Ensemble MD7 at UNICUM Festival in Slovenia and Trieste Primo Festival in Italy in 2010.
She is a professor at the Faculty of Education, Kumamoto University and a member of the Japan Society for Contemporary Music and the 21st Century Composer's Association.
http://www.harue-kunieda.com

皆様へのお願い

楽譜や歌詞・音楽書などの出版物を権利者に無断で複製（コピー）することは、著作権の侵害（私的利用など特別な場合を除く）にあたり、著作権法により罰せられます。また、出版物からの不法なコピーが行われますと、出版社は正常な出版活動が困難となり、ついには皆様方が必要とされるものもが出版できなくなります。
音楽出版社と日本音楽著作権協会（JASRAC）は、著作者の権利を守り、なおいっそう優れた作品の出版普及に全力をあげて努力してまいります。どうか不法コピーの防止に、皆様方のご協力をお願い申し上げます。

株式会社 音楽之友社
一般社団法人 日本音楽著作権協会

〈現代日本の音楽〉
セラフィム　ヴァイオリンとオーケストラのための

2017年3月31日　第1刷発行

作曲者　国枝　春恵
発行者　堀内久美雄
　　　　東京都新宿区神楽坂6の30
発行所　株式会社 音楽之友社
　　　　電話 03(3235)2111(代) 〒162-8716
　　　　http://www.ongakunotomo.co.jp/
　　　　振替 00170-4-196250

490952

落丁本・乱丁本はお取替いたします。
Printed in Japan.

組版：㈱ホッタガクフ
印刷／製本：㈱平河工業社

※この出版物は、「熊本大学学術出版助成」による助成を受けています。